FOCUS ON GRAMMAR
AN INTEGRATED SKILLS APPROACH

THIRD EDITION

MARJORIE FUCHS
MARGARET BONNER

WITH JANE CURTIS

PEARSON
Longman

FOCUS ON GRAMMAR 4A: An Integrated Skills Approach
Workbook

Copyright © 2006, 2000, 1995 by Pearson Education, Inc.
All rights reserved.
No part of this publication may be reproduced,
stored in a retrieval system, or transmitted
in any form or by any means, electronic, mechanical,
photocopying, recording, or otherwise,
without the prior permission of the publisher.

Pearson Education, 10 Bank Street, White Plains, NY 10606

Staff credits: The people who made up the *Focus on Grammar 4 Workbook* team, representing editorial, production, design, and manufacturing, are listed below: Rhea Banker, Aerin Csigay, Karen Davy, Christine Edmonds, Nancy Flaggman, Ann France, Diana George, Laura Le Dréan, and Kathleen Silloway.
Cover images: Large shell, background, Nick Koudis, RF; large shell, center image, Kaz Chiba; background, Comstock Images, RF
Text design: Quorum Creative Services, Rhea Banker
Text composition: ElectraGraphics, Inc.
Text font: 11/13 Sabon, 10/13 Myriad Roman
Illustrator: Steven Schulman, p. 137.
Text credits: **p. 65**, Francine Klagsbrun, *Married People: Staying Together in the Age of Divorce.* New York: Bantam Books, 1985; **p. 68**, Eva Hoffman, *Lost in Translation: A Life in a New Language.* New York: Penguin, 1989; Ben Fong-Torres, *The Rice Room.* New York: Hyperion, 1994; Erich Von Däniken, *Chariots of the Gods?* New York: G.P. Putnam, 1977; **p. 69**, Antoine de Saint-Exupéry, *The Little Prince.* New York: Harcourt Brace, 1943; Margaret Mead, *Male and Female.* New York: William Morrow, 1949; Jay Matthews, *Escalante: The Best Teacher in America.* New York: Henry Holt, 1988; p. 70, Jean M. Auel, *The Clan of the Cave Bear.* New York: Crown, 1980; **p. 84**, Michael D. Lemonick, "Secrets of the Maya," *Time*, August 9, 1993; **pp. 119 and 122**, Maxine P. Fisher, *Walt Disney.* New York: Franklin Watts, 1988; **p. 123**, *Bottom Line Personal*, June 15, 1993. From an interview with Bob Sehlinger, author of *The Unofficial Guide to Walt Disney World and EPCOT*, 1993 edition. New York: Prentice Hall Travel; **p. 125**, Lisa Davis, "A Doubtful Device," *Health*, October, 1992, **pp. 92–95**.
Photo credits: **p. 6** PictureQuest; **p. 16** Kimberly White/Reuters/Corbis; **p. 21** Bettmann/Corbis; **p. 39** Getty Images; **p. 50** JLP/Deimos/Corbis; **p. 56** Atta Kenare/Getty Images; **p. 60** Jon Feingersh/zefa/Corbis; **p. 75** AP/Wide World Photos; **p. 119** General Photographic Agency/Getty Images; **p. 121** Bettmann/Corbis; **p. 141** Paul J. Richards/Getty Images.

ISBN: 0-13-191242-9 (Workbook A)

LONGMAN ON THE WEB

Longman.com offers online resources for teachers and students. Access our Companion Websites, our online catalog, and our local offices around the world.

Visit us at **longman.com**.

Printed in the United States of America
3 4 5 6 7 8 9 10—BAH—12 11 10 09 08 07 06

Contents

Part I: Present and Past: Review and Expansion
    Unit 1 Simple Present and Present Progressive   1
    Unit 2 Simple Past and Past Progressive   5
    Unit 3 Simple Past, Present Perfect, and Present Perfect Progressive   9
    Unit 4 Past Perfect and Past Perfect Progressive   15

Part II: Future: Review and Expansion
    Unit 5 Future and Future Progressive   24
    Unit 6 Future Perfect and Future Perfect Progressive   29

Part III: Negative Questions and Tag Questions, Additions and Responses
    Unit 7 Negative *Yes/No* Questions and Tag Questions   34
    Unit 8 *So, Too, Neither, Not either,* and *But*   39

Part IV: Gerunds and Infinitives
    Unit 9 Gerunds and Infinitives: Review and Expansion   43
    Unit 10 *Make, Have, Let, Help,* and *Get*   50

Part V: Phrasal Verbs
    Unit 11 Phrasal Verbs: Review   55
    Unit 12 Phrasal Verbs: Separable and Inseparable   59

Part VI: Adjective Clauses
    Unit 13 Adjective Clauses with Subject Relative Pronouns   64
    Unit 14 Adjective Clauses with Object Relative Pronouns or *When* and *Where*   68

Workbook Answer Key   AK-1

Tests
Units 1–4   T-1
Units 5–6   T-3
Units 7–8   T-5
Units 9–10   T-8
Units 11–12   T-10
Units 13–14   T-12

Answer Key for Tests   T-14

About the Authors

Marjorie Fuchs has taught ESL at New York City Technical College and LaGuardia Community College of the City University of New York and EFL at the Sprach Studio Lingua Nova in Munich, Germany. She holds a master's degree in Applied English Linguistics and a Certificate in TESOL from the University of Wisconsin–Madison. She has authored and co-authored many widely used books and multimedia materials, notably **Crossroads, Top Twenty ESL Word Games: Beginning Vocabulary Development, Families: Ten Card Games for Language Learners,** Focus on Grammar 3 and **4: An Integrated Skills Approach, Focus on Grammar 3** and **4 CD-ROM, Longman English Interactive 3** and **4, Grammar Express Basic, Grammar Express Basic CD-ROM, Grammar Express Intermediate,** and the workbooks to the **Longman Dictionary of American English,** the **Longman Photo Dictionary, The Oxford Picture Dictionary, Focus on Grammar 3,** and **Grammar Express Basic.**

Margaret Bonner has taught ESL at Hunter College and the Borough of Manhattan Community College of the City University of New York, at Taiwan National University in Taipei, and at Virginia Commonwealth University in Richmond. She holds a master's degree in Library Science from Columbia University; and she has done work toward a Ph.D. in English Literature at the Graduate Center of the City University of New York. She has authored and co-authored numerous ESL and EFL print and multimedia materials, including textbooks for the national school system of Oman, **Step into Writing: A Basic Writing Text,** Focus on Grammar 3 and **4: An Integrated Skills Approach, Grammar Express Basic CD-ROM, Grammar Express Basic Workbook, Grammar Express Intermediate, Focus on Grammar 3** and **4 CD-ROM, Longman English Interactive 4,** and **The Oxford Picture Dictionary Intermediate Workbook.**

Jane Curtis began teaching ESOL in Spain, where she participated in a Fulbright exchange program between the University of Barcelona and the University of Illinois at Urbana-Champaign. She currently teaches at Roosevelt University in Chicago, Illinois. She holds a master's degree in Spanish from the University of Illinois at Urbana-Champaign and a master's degree in Applied Linguistics from Northeastern Illinois University.

Simple Present and Present Progressive

UNIT 1

1 | SPELLING: SIMPLE PRESENT AND PRESENT PROGRESSIVE

Write the correct forms of the verbs.

Base Form	Simple Present Third-Person Singular	Present Participle
1. answer	answers	answering
2. _____	asks	_____
3. buy	_____	_____
4. _____	_____	coming
5. _____	does	_____
6. eat	_____	_____
7. _____	_____	employing
8. _____	_____	flying
9. forget	_____	_____
10. _____	has	_____
11. hurry	_____	_____
12. _____	_____	lying
13. open	_____	_____
14. rain	_____	_____
15. reach	_____	_____
16. _____	says	_____
17. tie	_____	_____
18. _____	_____	traveling

2 | SIMPLE PRESENT AND PRESENT PROGRESSIVE

Complete the conversations with the correct form of the verbs in parentheses—simple present or present progressive. Use contractions when possible.

A. **AMBER:** I _____think_____ I've seen you before. _____ you
   1. (think)
   _____ Professor Bertolucci's course this semester?
   2. (take)

   NOËL: No, but my twin sister, Dominique, _____ Italian this year.
   3. (study)

   AMBER: That _____ her! I _____ her name now. You two
   4. (be) 5. (remember)
   _____ exactly alike.
   6. (look)

B. **JARED:** _____ you _____ that woman over there?
   1. (know)

   TARO: That's Mangena. She usually _____ a pronunciation class at the
   2. (teach)
   Institute, but she _____ in the computer lab this term.
   3. (work)

   JARED: That's an interesting name. What _____ it _____?
   4. (mean)

   TARO: I'm not sure. I _____ I've ever known anyone else with that name.
   5. (not believe)

C. **ROSA:** How _____ you _____ your name?
   1. (spell)

   ZHUŌ: Here, I'll write it down for you.

   ROSA: You _____ unusual handwriting. It _____ very artistic.
   2. (have) 3. (look)

D. **IVY:** Hi. Why _____ you _____ there with such a terrible look
   1. (sit)
   on your face? You _____ too happy.
   2. (not seem)

   LEE: I _____ to read this letter from my friend. He _____
   3. (try) 4. (not like)
   to use a computer, so he _____ his letters by hand and his handwriting
   5. (write)
   _____ awful. It _____ to get on my nerves.
   6. (be) 7. (begin)

E. **AMY:** _____ you _____ to hear something interesting? Justin
   1. (want)
   _____ to become a graphologist.
   2. (study)

   CHRIS: What exactly _____ a graphologist _____?
   3. (do)

   AMY: A graphologist _____ people's handwriting. You can learn a lot about
   4. (analyze)
   people from the way they _____—especially from how they
   5. (write)
   _____ their name.
   6. (sign)

3 | SIMPLE PRESENT AND PRESENT PROGRESSIVE

Complete this article. Use the correct form of the verbs in parentheses—simple present or present progressive. Sometimes there is more than one correct answer.

Right now Pam O'Neil __is taking__ a test, but she __doesn't know__ it. She
1. (take)   2. (not know)

_____ on what she _____—not on how her handwriting
3. (focus)   4. (write)

_____. The person who will analyze the test is a graphologist—someone
5. (look)

who _____ handwriting. Graphologists _____ that a
     6. (study)   7. (believe)

person's handwriting _____ an indication of his or her personality and
                               8. (give)

character. These days, many businesses _____ graphologists to help them
                                              9. (use)

decide who to hire.

    What exactly _____ company graphologist Perry Vance _____
                                                                                     10. (hope)

to learn from applicants' writing samples? "I always _____ for clues to possible
                                                        11. (look)

behavior," he explained. "For example, the slant of the writing usually _____ a
                                                                         12. (tell)

lot. _____ the writing _____ to the left or to the right? A left slant
                                            13. (lean)

often _____ a shy personality. The position of the sample on the page is also
         14. (indicate)

important," Vance continued. "The right-hand margin of the page _____ the
                                                                   15. (represent)

future. Here's a writing sample from an executive who right now _____ a new
                                                                        16. (plan)

direction for a large company. Notice that this person _____ much room in the
                                                                17. (not leave)

right-hand margin. This is the writing of someone who never _____ looking at
                                                                     18. (avoid)

the future."

    "What about signatures?" I asked. "Yes, signatures _____ us a lot about
                                                        19. (show)

someone," said Vance. "Look at this one by a chief executive officer of a large firm. He

_____ in the news a lot these days because the government _____
20. (be)   21. (investigate)

his company. Those very large strokes are typical of a person who _____ about
                                                                22. (think)

himself first and _____ advantage of other people." Vance always
                         23. (take)

_____, however, that his analysis _____ an applicant's future job
24. (warn)   25. (not guarantee)

performance. There's no substitute for careful review of a complete application.

4 | EDITING

Read this e-mail from a student to her favorite English teacher. There are ten mistakes in the use of the simple present and the present progressive. The first mistake is already corrected. Find and correct nine more.

Hi!

    Well, I'm here at my new school, and ~~I'm liking~~ *I like* it very much. I'm study English this semester, but the classes are really different from our English classes in Korea. My teachers doesn't know how to speak Korean, and my classmates are coming from countries all around the world, so we use English all the time. That is meaning that I'm getting a lot of good practice these days.

    Although I'm very happy, I'm sometimes having problems. I'm not understand my classmates' names because they don't look or sound like Korean names. I always ask the same questions: "What's your name?" and "How you spell it?" My teachers want me to call them by their first names. It's difficult for me to treat my teachers so informally, but I trying. Slowly but surely, I'm getting accustomed to my life here.

    I miss you a lot. Your still my favorite English teacher.

Hye Lee

Simple Past and Past Progressive

UNIT 2

1 | SPELLING: REGULAR AND IRREGULAR SIMPLE PAST FORMS

Write the correct forms of the verbs.

Base Form	Simple Past
1. agree	agreed
2. _____	applied
3. be	_____ OR _____
4. become	_____
5. carry	_____
6. develop	_____
7. _____	ate
8. fall	_____
9. _____	felt
10. get	_____
11. grow	_____
12. live	_____
13. _____	met
14. _____	paid
15. permit	_____
16. plan	_____
17. _____	sent
18. sleep	_____

2 | SIMPLE PAST AND PAST PROGRESSIVE

Complete this magazine article. Use the correct form of the verbs in parentheses—simple past or past progressive. Sometimes there is more than one correct answer.

First Meetings
by Rebecca Hubbard

What ___were___ you ___doing___ (1. do) when you first _____ (2. meet) that special person in your life? A few months ago, we _____ (3. ask) some couples to tell us about themselves. _____ (4. be) it love at first sight, or _____ you hardly _____ (5. notice) each other? _____ you _____ (6. go) out with someone else before you _____ (7. find) your One True Love? Read some of the great stories from our readers.

Dana and I sure _____ (8. not fall) in love at first sight! We _____ (9. work) in the same office when we _____ (10. meet). At the time the company _____ (11. hire) me, she _____ (12. try) to get a promotion. It _____ (13. be) my first job. I _____ (14. feel) scared, so I _____ (15. pretend) to know everything. Of course Dana _____ (16. think) I _____ (17. want) to get the promotion instead of her. One day I _____ (18. work) on a problem when she _____ (19. come) into my office. I _____ (20. not ask) her for help at first, but I was stuck, so finally I did. And guess what! She _____ (21. solve) the problem! So then we _____ (22. stop) competing with each other and _____ (23. fall) in love instead.

Van and I _____ the same high school social studies class when we
24. (take)

_____. We _____ friends right away. At the time, I _____
25. (meet)   26. (become)   27. (date)

someone else, and Van _____ interested in a romantic relationship. One day the
28. (not seem)

teacher _____ me while I _____ to Van. The teacher _____
29. (hear)   30. (whisper)   31. (get)

angry at us for talking during class, and she _____ both of us to stay after
32. (tell)

school. I _____ to complain about such a severe punishment, but then I
33. (want)

_____ my mind because I _____ that staying late with a good friend
34. (change)   35. (realize)

might be fun. That afternoon, Van and I _____ talking. I was right. As soon as I
36. (not stop)

_____ with my old boyfriend, Van _____ me out.
37. (break up)   38. (ask)

Aleesha _____ into the apartment next door when I _____ her
39. (move)   40. (see)

for the first time. I _____ on the front steps while she _____ to park a
41. (sit)   42. (try)

U-Haul moving truck in front of the apartment building. As soon as she _____
43. (jump)

out of the truck, I _____, "I'm going to marry that woman." I _____
44. (think)   45. (not ask)

her out right away because a guy _____ her move. He _____ like her
46. (help)   47. (seem)

boyfriend. One day I _____ Aleesha and her "boyfriend" in the hall. She
48. (see)

_____ me to her brother! I _____ her to dinner the next weekend.
49. (introduce)   50. (invite)

3 | EDITING

Read this entry from Aleesha's journal. There are nine mistakes in the use of the simple past and the past progressive. The first mistake is already corrected. Find and correct eight more.

December 16

    I'm really glad that I ~~was deciding~~ *decided* to rent this apartment. I almost wasn't move here because the rent is a little high, but I'm happy to be here. All the other apartments I looked at were seeming so small, and the neighborhoods just weren't as beautiful as this one. And moving wasn't as bad as I feared. My original plan was to take a week off from work, but when Hakim was offering to help, I didn't need so much time. What a great brother! We were moving everything into the apartment in two days. The man next door was really nice to us. On the second day, he even helped Hakim with some of the heavy furniture. His name is Jared. I don't even unpack the kitchen stuff last weekend because I was so tired. Last night I walking Mitzi for only two blocks. When I came back, Jared stood downstairs. I think I made him nervous because he was dropping his mail when he saw me. I'd like to ask him over for coffee this weekend (in order to thank him), but everything is still in boxes. Maybe in a couple of weeks . . .

Simple Past, Present Perfect, and Present Perfect Progressive

UNIT 3

1 | SPELLING: SIMPLE PAST AND PRESENT PERFECT

Write the correct forms of the verbs.

Base Form	Simple Past	Past Participle
1. become	became	become
2. bring		
3. choose		
4. delay		
5. feel		
6. find		
7. finish		
8. get		
9. graduate		
10. hide		
11. notice		
12. omit		
13. own		
14. read		
15. reply		
16. rip		
17. show		
18. speak		

2 | CONTRAST: SIMPLE PAST, PRESENT PERFECT, AND PRESENT PERFECT PROGRESSIVE

Look at the reporter's notes about the bride's and the groom's families. Then write statements about them, using the words in parentheses. Use the simple past, present perfect, or present perfect progressive form of the verbs. Add any necessary words to the time expressions. Sometimes there is more than one correct answer.

THE SKOAP-POHLIG WEDDING
BACKGROUND INFORMATION

Bride	Groom
Nakisha Skoap	Simon Pohlig
born in Broadfield	moved to Broadfield in 1997
lived here all her life	bought Sharney's Restaurant in 1999
B.A., Claremont College, 1999	basketball coach for Boys and Girls Club
1996—Began working for Broadfield Examiner	2002–2004 author, Simon Says and Duck Soup, kids' cookbooks
2002—became crime news reporter and started master's degree program in political science	in Jan., started developing local TV show
started research on crime in schools in Jan.	Mother—Tina Pohlig, president of TLC Meals, Inc. for two years, but plans to retire soon
Father—James Skoap, joined the Broadfield Police Department in 1984, retired in 2004	

1. (Nakisha Skoap / live in Broadfield / all her life)

   Nakisha Skoap has lived in Broadfield all her life.

2. (she / graduate / from college / 1999)

3. (report / crime news / 2002)

4. (recently, / research / crime in schools)

5. (work / on her master's degree / 2002)

6. (her father / work / for the Broadfield Police Department / 20 years)

7. (Simon Pohlig / move / to Broadfield / 1997)

8. (own / Sharney's Restaurant / 1999)

9. (coach / basketball / for the Boys and Girls Club / two years)

10. (write / two cookbooks for children)

11. (plan / a local television show / several months)

12. (the groom's mother / serve / as the president of TLC Meals, Inc. / two years)

3 | SIMPLE PAST, PRESENT PERFECT, AND PRESENT PERFECT PROGRESSIVE

Look at Nakisha's job application. Then complete the personnel officer's notes. Use the correct affirmative or negative form of the verbs in parentheses—simple past, present perfect, or present perfect progressive. Sometimes there is more than one correct answer.

CODEX MAGAZINE
JOB APPLICATION

1. Position applied for: _Editor_ Today's date: _Nov. 12, 2004_
2. Full legal name _Skoap-Pohlig_   _Nakisha_   _Ann_
   Last   First   Middle
3. Current address _22 East 10th Street_

   Broadfield,   _Ohio_   _43216_   How long at this address? _5 months_
   City   State   Zip Code
4. Previous address _17 Willow Terrace_

   Broadfield,   _Ohio_   _43216_   How long at this address? _1973–June 1, 2004_
   City   State   Zip Code
5. Education. Circle the number of years of post high school education. 1 2 3 4 5 6 ⑦ 8
6.   Name of Institution   Degree   Major   Dates Attended

   1. _Claremont College_   _B.A._   _Journalism_   _1995–1999_

   2. _Ohio State University_   _—_   _Urban Studies_   _2001_

   3. _Ohio State University_   _Political Science_ _2002–present_

   If you expect to complete an educational program soon, indicate the date and type of program.

   I expect to receive my M.S. in political science in January.

7. Current job. May we contact your present supervisor? ____ yes _x_ no

   Job Title _Reporter_   Employer _Broadfield Examiner_

   Type of Business _newspaper_   Address _1400 River Street, Broadfield, OH 43216_

   Dates (month/year) _9/96_   to (month/year) _present_

8. In your own handwriting, describe your duties and what you find most satisfying in this job.

   I am currently a crime reporter for a daily newspaper. I write local crime news.

   I especially enjoy working with my supervisor.

Simple Past, Present Perfect, and Present Perfect Progressive | 13

1. I ___have interviewed___ Nakisha Skoap-Pohlig for the editorial position.
   (interview)
2. She _____ for a job on November 12.
   (apply)
3. She _____ at the *Broadfield Examiner* for a long time.
   (work)
4. She _____ several excellent articles for that publication.
   (write)
5. She _____ that job while she _____ a college student.
   (find)   (be)
6. She _____ two schools of higher education.
   (attend)
7. She _____ classes at Claremont College in 1995 and _____
   (begin)   (receive)
   her B.A. there.
8. Then she _____ to Ohio State University.
   (go on)
9. She _____ classes in two different departments at Ohio State.
   (take)
10. She _____ a master's program in urban studies.
    (start)
11. She _____ a degree in urban studies, though.
    (get)
12. After a year, she _____ to study political science instead.
    (decide)
13. She _____ her master's degree yet.
    (receive)
14. She _____ at Willow Terrace most of her life.
    (live)
15. For the past five months, she _____ on East 10th Street.
    (live)
16. The company graphologist _____ that we contact this applicant very soon
    (recommend)
    for another interview.
17. He says that in question 8 of the application, Ms. Skoap-Pohlig _____ a space
    (leave)
    between some words when she mentioned her supervisor.
18. He feels that this means she probably _____ her supervisor yet about looking
    (tell)
    for a new job.
19. When Ms. Skoap-Pohlig answered question 8, she _____ her writing to either
    (slant)
    the left or the right.
20. The graphologist _____ to me yesterday that this indicates that she is a clear
    (explain)
    and independent thinker.

4 | EDITING

Read this letter to an advice column. There are fourteen mistakes in the use of the simple past, present perfect, and present perfect progressive. The first mistake is already corrected. Find and correct thirteen more.

Dear John,

    My son and his girlfriend have ~~made~~ *been making* wedding plans for the past few months. At first I was delighted, but last week I have heard something that changed my feelings. It seems that our future daughter-in-law has been deciding to keep her own last name after the wedding. Her reasons: First, she doesn't want to "lose her identity." Her parents have named her 31 years ago, and she was Donna Esposito since then. She sees no reason to change now. Second, she is a member of the Rockland Symphony Orchestra and she performed with them for eight years. As a result, she already became known professionally by her maiden name.

    John, when I've gotten married, I didn't think of keeping my maiden name. I have felt so proud when I became "Mrs. Smith." We named our son after my father, but our surname showed that we three were a family.

    I've been reading two articles about this trend, and I can now understand her decision to use her maiden name professionally. But I still can't understand why she wants to use it socially.

    My husband and I have been trying many times to hide our hurt feelings, but it's been getting harder. I want to tell her and my son what I think, but my husband says it's none of our business.

    My son didn't say anything so far, so we don't know how he feels. Have we been making the right choice by keeping quiet?

                        A Concerned Mother Who Hasn't Been Saying One Word Yet

Past Perfect and Past Perfect Progressive

UNIT 4

1 | SPELLING: REGULAR AND IRREGULAR PAST PARTICIPLES

Write the correct forms of the verbs.

Base Form	Present Participle	Past Participle
1. bet	betting	bet
2. _____	breaking	_____
3. cut	_____	_____
4. do	_____	_____
5. entertain	_____	_____
6. _____	_____	fought
7. forgive	_____	_____
8. lead	_____	_____
9. plan	_____	_____
10. practice	_____	_____
11. quit	_____	_____
12. _____	_____	sought
13. _____	_____	sunk
14. steal	_____	_____
15. sweep	_____	_____
16. swim	_____	_____
17. tell	_____	_____
18. _____	_____	withdrawn

2 | PAST PERFECT: AFFIRMATIVE AND NEGATIVE STATEMENTS

Read this article about Arnold Schwarzenegger. Complete the information with the affirmative or negative past perfect form of the verbs in parentheses.

Action Hero and More

Arnold Schwarzenegger is an example of what people can accomplish with determination and hard work. He was just six years old when he decided to become a famous athlete. His father __had taken__ him to a special event
1. (take)
featuring Olympic swimming champion Johnny Weissmuller, and Schwarzenegger felt that one day he too would be a champion. When he first arrived in the United States in 1968, he _____ already _____ several bodybuilding competitions in
2. (win)
Europe, but no one imagined that a bodybuilder from Austria could become a famous movie star, a successful businessman, and the governor of California.

Because Schwarzenegger _____ much English, he had a lot of problems
3. (learn)
communicating when he got to the United States. He _____ much money
4. (bring)
with him either, but that didn't stop him. Before long, he _____ a sponsor
5. (find)
so that he could continue his training as a bodybuilder, and he _____ even
_____ his own business selling supplies to other athletes. By 1970, he
6. (establish)
_____ the title of "Mr. Olympia," and some Hollywood producers
7. (earn)
_____ him the movie role of Hercules. Schwarzenegger appeared in
8. (offer)

movies and on television throughout the 1970s and continued winning bodybuilding championships. By the time the decade was over, he _____ also _____ a best-selling book and he _____ a B.A. in business
9. (write)   10. (receive)

and international economics from the University of Wisconsin. He _____
11. (get)

married yet, but he _____ Maria Shriver, his future wife. After spending
12. (meet)

time with Shriver's family, Schwarzenegger got involved with the Special Olympics, an organization founded by his mother-in-law, Eunice Kennedy Shriver, to provide sports training and athletic competition for people with disabilities.

Schwarzenegger achieved even greater success in the 1980s and 1990s. By the mid-1980s, he _____ in *Conan the Barbarian* and *The Terminator*. He then
13. (star)

filmed action movies such as *Commando, Predator, The Running Man,* and *Red Heat.* Before the end of the decade, Schwarzenegger _____ the first Planet Hollywood
14. (open)

restaurant along with fellow action stars Bruce Willis and Sylvester Stallone. He

_____ one of the wealthiest and most popular actors in Hollywood. In the
15. (become)

1990s, he made more action films and more comedies like *Kindergarten Cop* and *Junior.* He also served as chairman of the President's Council on Physical Fitness, worked on other volunteer projects, and seemed to be increasingly interested in politics.

Before announcing his plans to run for governor of California in July 2003, Schwarzenegger _____ filming *Terminator 3: Rise of the Machines.* He started
16. (finish)

his new job as California's chief executive on November 17 of that year.

The question now is: What's next for Arnold?

3 | PAST PERFECT: YES/NO QUESTIONS AND SHORT ANSWERS

Look at a day in the life of a busy governor. Complete the questions about his day and give short answers. Use the past perfect.

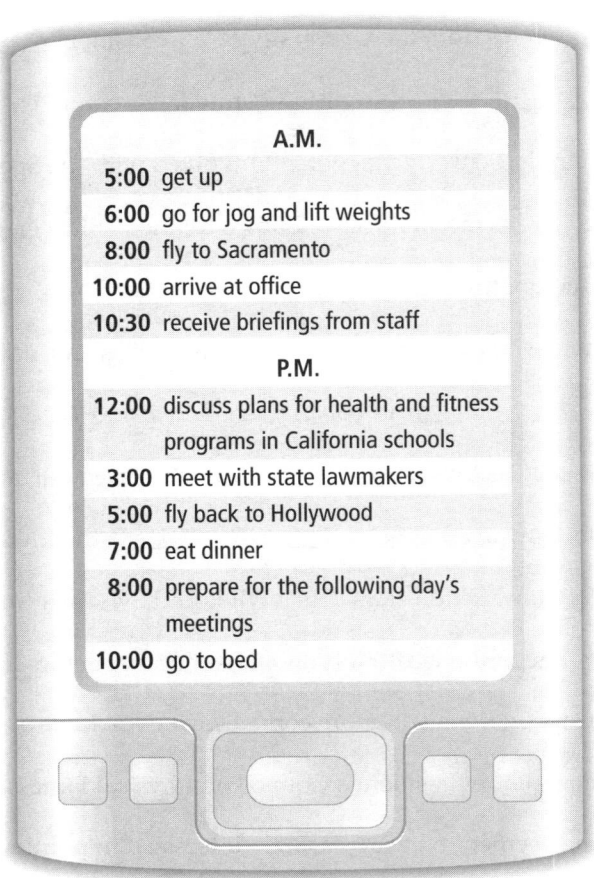

1. It was 6:00 A.M.

    A: _____Had he gotten up_____ yet?

    B: _____Yes, he had._____

2. The governor was going for his morning jog.

    A: _____ to Sacramento yet?

    B: _____

3. It was 9:00 A.M.

    A: _____ at his office by then?

    B: _____

4. It was noon.

   A: _____ briefings from his staff yet?

   B: _____

5. It was shortly before 5:00 in the afternoon.

   A: _____ with state lawmakers?

   B: _____

6. At 6:30 in the evening, the governor arrived in Hollywood.

   A: _____ dinner yet?

   B: _____

7. At 10:00 P.M., he went to bed.

   A: _____ for meetings the following day?

   B: _____

4 | PAST PERFECT PROGRESSIVE: AFFIRMATIVE AND NEGATIVE STATEMENTS

Read the situations. Draw conclusions, using the affirmative or negative past perfect progressive form of the correct verbs from the box.

cry	do	drink	eat	laugh
listen	pay	rain	wash	~~watch~~

1. Mara wasn't in the living room, but the TV was on and there was a movie in the DVD player.

   She _____*had been watching*_____ the Arnold Schwarzenegger comedy *Twins*.

2. The lights were off, and none of her schoolbooks were around.

   She _____ homework.

3. The window was open, and the floor was a little wet.

   It _____.

4. There was half a sandwich on the coffee table.

   Mara _____ the sandwich.

5. There was an unopened bottle of soda next to the sandwich.

   She _____ the soda.

(continued)

6. Mara entered the room. There were tears on her face.

   At first I thought she _____.

7. I was wrong. Mara wasn't upset.

   She _____ really hard because of what was happening in the movie.

8. There was a stack of clean plates in the kitchen sink.

   She _____ dishes.

9. Mara could hear the TV from the kitchen.

   She _____ to the movie from the kitchen.

10. I was surprised when I realized how late it was.

    I _____ attention to the time.

5 | PAST PERFECT PROGRESSIVE: QUESTIONS

*A group of film students is planning the questions that they will ask a famous actor-director after he gives a lecture at their university. Use **when** and the words in parentheses to write questions with the past perfect progressive.*

1. He made his first major film. (he / dream of stardom for a long time)

   Had he been dreaming of stardom for a long time when he made his first major film?

2. He finally found an acting job. (How long / he / live in Hollywood)

   _____

3. He became a successful actor. (he / really work as a cook in a fast-food restaurant)

   _____

4. He decided to enroll in classes at the Actors Studio Drama School. (Where / he / study)

   _____

5. He began his acting classes. (Why / he / take courses in accounting)

   _____

6. He directed his first film. (How long / he / think about working behind the cameras)

   _____

7. He started his own production company. (he / look for investors for a long time)

   _____

6 | PAST PERFECT AND PAST PERFECT PROGRESSIVE

Complete this passage. Use the past perfect or past perfect progressive form of the verbs in parentheses. Use the progressive form when possible.

An Action Star of Yesteryear

Johnny Weissmuller became famous playing Tarzan in a number of movies in the 1930s and '40s. However, his first success ____had been____ as a swimmer.
1. (be)

Weissmuller was born in Romania, but he later claimed to be from a small town in western Pennsylvania— probably because he _____ to try out
2. (decide)

for the U.S. Olympic team. He _____
3. (swim)

for most of his life and went on to win five gold medals in the 1924 and 1928 Olympics and dozens of amateur and professional championships. When he ended his career as a swimmer, he _____ never _____ a race.
4. (lose)

Although he _____ only small roles, Johnny Weissmuller got the role of Tarzan
5. (have)

in the 1932 movie *Tarzan the Ape Man*. MGM studio executives _____ for an
6. (search)

actor to star in their movie but _____ what they were looking for. Then they
7. (not find)

heard about Weissmuller, who _____ as a swimsuit and underwear model. He
8. (work)

got the job because of his physical appearance and abilities, not because of his acting skills. Nevertheless, *Tarzan the Ape Man* was a hit. Audiences loved watching the adventures of the man who _____ in the jungle since he was a young boy, and they loved Johnny
9. (live)

Weissmuller. By 1948, he _____ in a total of 12 Tarzan films. As he got older,
10. (appear)

Weissmuller could no longer play roles like Tarzan. After he _____ movies for
11. (make)

more than 20 years, he retired from films and went into business, but audiences still remembered him as the "King of the Jungle."

7 | SIMPLE PAST AND PAST PERFECT IN TIME CLAUSES

Look at some important events in Jennifer Lopez's life and career. Determine the correct order of the phrases below. Then combine the phrases and use the past perfect or past perfect progressive to express the event that happened first. Use the progressive form when possible. Use the simple past for the event that happened second. Add commas when necessary.

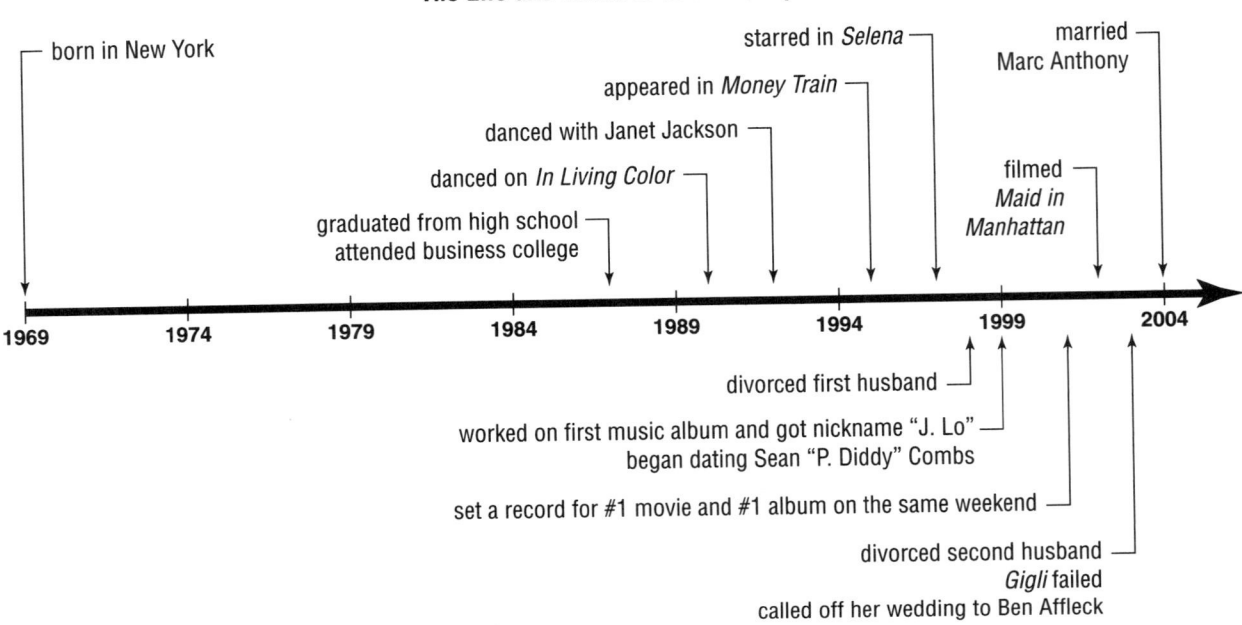

1. briefly attended business college / graduated from high school

   After *Jennifer Lopez had graduated from high school, she briefly attended business college.*

2. became a professional dancer / studied at a business college

   Before _____

3. danced with Janet Jackson / was a dancer on the popular TV show *In Living Color*

   _____ before _____

4. appeared in her first major film / danced professionally for several years

   By the time _____

5. starred in *Selena* / finished the action film *Money Train*

   When _____ already _____

6. started her singing career / divorced her first husband

   _____ by the time _____

7. got the name "J. Lo" / made several films

   _____ before _____

8. set a record for #1 movie and #1 album on the same weekend / dated Sean "P. Diddy" Combs

   When _____

9. filmed *Maid in Manhattan* / ended her relationship with her second husband

   When _____ yet.

10. fell in love with Ben Affleck / got married twice

    By the time _____ already _____

11. called off her wedding to Ben Affleck / their movie *Gigli* failed at the box office

    _____ by the time _____

12. called off her wedding to Ben Affleck / married actor and singer Marc Anthony

    _____ after _____

UNIT 5

PART II Future: Review and Expansion

Future and Future Progressive

1 | CONTRAST OF FUTURE FORMS

Circle the best words to complete these conversations between two neighbors.

1. **A:** Hi, Jan. What are you doing?

   B: Packing. We'll move / (We're moving) tomorrow.

2. **A:** Do you need any help?

   B: Well, actually, I could use a hand.

   A: OK. I'll come / I'm going to come over right away.

3. **A:** Do you take / Are you taking the refrigerator?

   B: No. Our new house already has one.

4. **A:** I can't reach that vase.

   B: No problem. I'm handing / I'll hand it to you.

5. **A:** Watch out! It'll fall / It's going to fall!

   B: Don't worry. I've got it.

6. **A:** You're moving / You'll move out of state, right?

   B: Yes. To Boston.

7. **A:** Are you driving / Do you drive there?

   B: No. We'll fly / We're flying.

8. **A:** How are you getting / do you get to the airport?

   B: We're going to take / We take a taxi.

9. **A:** Oh, don't take a taxi. I'm driving / I'll drive you.

   B: Thank you! I hope we're having / we're going to have neighbors as nice as you in our new neighborhood!

2 | FUTURE PROGRESSIVE: AFFIRMATIVE AND NEGATIVE STATEMENTS

Complete this article. Use the affirmative or negative future progressive form of the words in parentheses.

An Old Approach to a New Problem

Next year, Azize and Kiral Yazgan __will be moving__ from their rented two-bedroom city apartment to a place called Glenn
1. (will / move)

Commons. There they _____ in one of a
2. (will / live)

row of houses facing other houses, all without fences or hedges. They

_____ their car in an area in back of the houses. And even though
3. (be going to / park)

there is a nice kitchen with a large window, the Yazgans _____
4. (be going to / prepare)

dinners there. Azize, Kiral, and their two children _____ most
5. (will / eat)

evening meals along with 20 other families in a common house. And they

_____ there. They _____ along paths and
6. (will / drive)   7. (will / walk)

greenery.

This doesn't sound like the suburbs. What's going on? The Yazgans, along with a growing

number of other people, _____ to one of the many planned
8. (will / move)

communities that are now being built around the world. Called "co-housing," these

communities have cooperative living arrangements that avoid some of the isolation and

loneliness of suburban life.

While the Yazgans get to know their neighbors, they _____ also

_____ money. For starters, they _____ a
9. (will / save)   10. (be going to / buy)

lawn mower or a washer-dryer since the community shares large equipment. And they

_____ food, utility, or child-care bills as individuals either.
11. (be going to / pay)

Child care? The Yazgans _____ anymore about what to do when
12. (will / worry)

one of their children has a cold and each parent is due at a business meeting in an hour. The

center _____ for that.
13. (will / provide)

(continued)

The Yazgans will, however, have some added responsibilities. For one thing, they will have to be much more involved in their community. Even before they move in, the couple _____ monthly meetings to decide how the community is run. And
14. (be going to / attend)
several times a month, they _____ to prepare the dinners and
15. (will / help)
_____ the child care for others. It's clearly not a lifestyle that will
16. (will / provide)
appeal to everyone.

Who started this new idea? Actually, the idea itself is quite old—going back to 19th-century European villages. Co-housing has been used in Denmark since 1972. Even though only a few co-housing communities have been completed in Canada, Europe, the United States, and New Zealand, we _____ more and more of them in the near future as
17. (be going to / see)
people try to improve the quality of their lives by returning to some of the values of the past.

3 | FUTURE PROGRESSIVE: QUESTIONS AND SHORT ANSWERS

Complete the conversations at a co-housing meeting. Use the future progressive form of the words in parentheses or short answers where appropriate.

1. **A:** When <u>will we be planting the garden</u>_____?
   (we / will / plant the garden)
   B: Jack has bought the seeds, so we should be ready to start this week.

2. **A:** Speaking of gardening, Martha, _____?
   (you / be going to / use the lawn mower / tomorrow)
   B: _____. You can have it if you'd like.

3. **A:** You know, with more families moving in, the laundry facilities aren't adequate anymore.

   When _____?
   (we / will / get new washers)
   B: The housing committee is getting information on brands and prices. They'll be ready to report on them at the next meeting.

4. **A:** Jack, _____?
   (you / will / go to the post office / tomorrow)
   B: _____. Can I mail something for you?

5. **A:** Eun, you and Bon-Hua are in charge of dinner Friday night. What _____?
   (you / be going to / make)

   B: How does vegetable soup, roast chicken, corn bread, salad, and chocolate chip cookies sound to you?

6. **A:** I really enjoyed that slide show last month. _____?
   (the entertainment committee / will / plan anything else in the near future)

   B: _____. We're thinking of organizing a dance over the holidays.

7. **A:** I was just looking at my calendar. The 15th of next month is a Sunday. _____?
   (we / be going to / meet / then)

   B: _____. We usually meet on the 15th, but when the 15th falls on a weekend, we switch the meeting to the following Monday.

4 | FUTURE PROGRESSIVE OR SIMPLE PRESENT

Look at Azize and Kiral Yazgan's schedules for tomorrow. Complete the statements. Use the correct form of the verbs—future progressive with **will** or simple present.

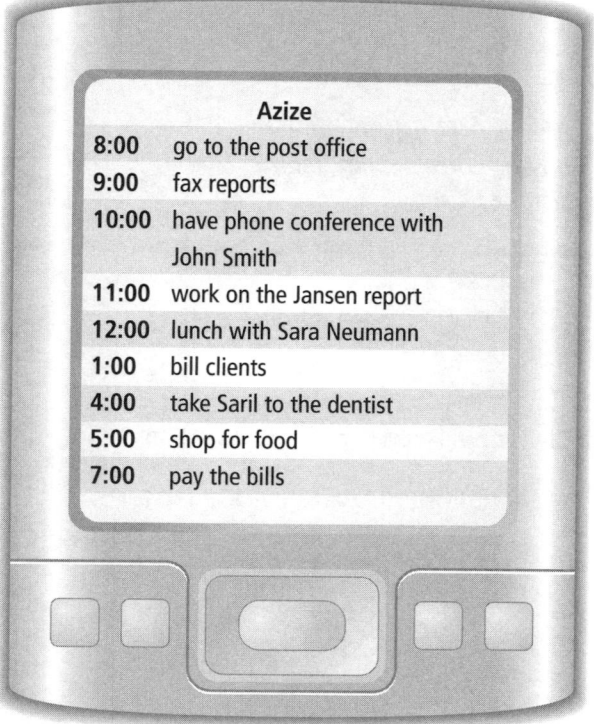
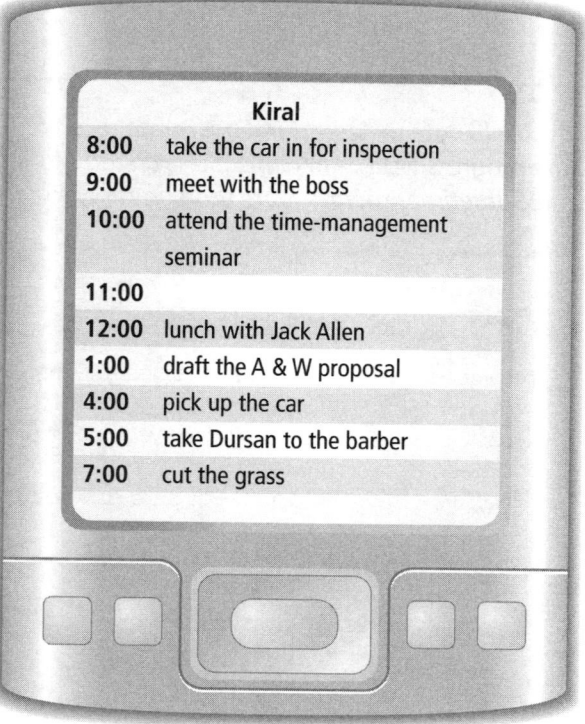

Azize	
8:00	go to the post office
9:00	fax reports
10:00	have phone conference with John Smith
11:00	work on the Jansen report
12:00	lunch with Sara Neumann
1:00	bill clients
4:00	take Saril to the dentist
5:00	shop for food
7:00	pay the bills

Kiral	
8:00	take the car in for inspection
9:00	meet with the boss
10:00	attend the time-management seminar
11:00	
12:00	lunch with Jack Allen
1:00	draft the A & W proposal
4:00	pick up the car
5:00	take Dursan to the barber
7:00	cut the grass

(continued)

1. While Azize _____ goes to _____ the post office, Kiral _____ will be taking the car in for inspection _____.

2. Kiral _____ his boss while Azize _____.

3. While Kiral _____ a time-management seminar, Azize _____.

4. While Azize _____ lunch with Sara Neumann, Kiral _____.

5. Azize _____ while Kiral _____ the A & W proposal.

6. While Kiral _____ the car, Azize _____.

7. Azize _____ food while Kiral _____.

8. While Azize _____ the bills, Kiral _____.

5 | EDITING

Read Kiral's note to Azize. Kiral has made seven mistakes in the use of the future and the future progressive. The first mistake is already corrected. Find and correct six more. (Note: Sometimes there is more than one way to correct a mistake.)

Azize—It's 8:00 p.m. now. ~~I go~~ I'm going to Jack's with the kids in a few minutes. We'll be play cards until 10:30 or so. While we'll play cards, Jack's daughter will be watching the kids. It will rain, so I closed all the windows. Don't forget to watch "CSI"! It'll start at 10:00. I call you after the card game because by the time we get home, you're sleeping. Enjoy your evening!

Love, K

UNIT 6

Future Perfect and Future Perfect Progressive

1 | AFFIRMATIVE AND NEGATIVE STATEMENTS

Complete this article. Use the correct form of the verbs in parentheses—future perfect or future perfect progressive.

As of December this year, Pam and Jessica Weiner ___will have been working___ as personal
1. (work)

time-management consultants for five years. Tired of disorganization at home, Pam and Jessica developed a system that worked so well that they started teaching it to others. By this anniversary celebration, hundreds of people _____
2. (complete)

the Weiners' seminars, and these efficient sisters _____
3. (help)

them manage the confusion in their personal lives.

"What a difference their seminars made!" exclaimed Corinne Smith, who completed the course a few years ago. "This December, I _____ their
4. (use)

system for two years. I used to do my holiday shopping on December 23. However, this year, I

_____ all my gifts by early November, and I
5. (buy)

_____ them too."
6. (wrap)

Why do we need a system? "Our lives are so complicated that we can't remember it all," explained Pam Weiner. "A good example is a new family in our seminar. Ana and Jon have two children, they both work, but they have no system. By Monday, they _____
7. (not plan)

the week's menu, and they _____ on a driving
8. (not decide)

(continued)

schedule for the week's activities. That means by the time Friday comes along, they _____ probably _____ for days about
9. (argue)
these things."

The Metcalfs, one of many satisfied families, feel that their life has improved a lot since they finished the seminars. "At the end of this week, we _____
10. (not waste)
our energy arguing about who does what in the house," Aida Metcalf told us. "And we can plan for fun activities. We know that we _____ all the
11. (complete)
housework by Saturday, and we can make plans to go out. When we go back to work on Monday, we _____ a good time for two days, and we'll
12. (have)
feel refreshed."

The system also works for long-range planning. "Before the seminars, our summers were a nightmare," Aida says. "We never did the things we wanted to do. But by the end of August this year, we _____ in our community yard sale and
13. (participate)
_____ the house. And I can be sure that we
14. (redecorate)
_____ all the preparations for our September family
15. (make)
get-together."

Children enjoy using the system too. "I made a calendar for Corrie, our 12-year-old," reported Arnie Metcalf. "She loves it. By the time she gets on the school bus tomorrow morning, she _____ several chores. For example, she
16. (do)
_____ her own room, and most likely she
17. (straighten)
_____ her own lunch as well."
18. (pack)

The Weiners are scheduled to appear on tomorrow's *Around Town*, and this also represents a kind of anniversary for them. "Our television appearances started with this show," Pam Weiner told us. "As of tomorrow, we _____ our system to
19. (explain)
television audiences for an entire year."

2 | QUESTIONS AND RESPONSES

Complete the conversations. Use the future perfect or future perfect progressive form of the words in parentheses or short answers where appropriate.

1. **A:** I'm going to the mall. Bye.

   B: I have to leave at two o'clock for a dentist appointment. <u>Will you have brought</u> (you / bring) the car back by then?

   A: _____. I don't have much to buy.

2. **A:** Corrie, your group is singing at the fund-raiser next weekend, right? By three o'clock, how long _____(you / perform)_____?

   B: About half an hour. Why?

   A: There's a rock band from the high school that wants to start at three.

3. **A:** This is Aida. I'm in charge of the handicrafts booth this year. How many of those nice dish towels _____ (you / sew) by Sunday? Do you know?

   B: Oh, at least 20.

4. **A:** Oh, no! I forgot about carpooling today.

   B: Suppose you leave right now. How long _____ (the kids / wait) by the time you get there?

   A: Only about 15 minutes. I guess that's not a big deal.

5. **A:** Arnie, _____ (the paint / dry) downstairs by tomorrow afternoon?

   B: _____. We'd better give it until tomorrow night. Why?

   A: I want to hang the curtains.

6. **A:** _____ (the cleaners / deliver) them by then?

   B: _____. They promised me I'd have them by noon.

7. **A:** Do you realize that September first is an anniversary? That's the date we moved into this house.

   B: How many years _____ (we / live) here?

   A: Ten. Can you believe it?

3 | QUESTIONS AND AFFIRMATIVE STATEMENTS

Look at the Metcalfs' calendar for August. Write questions about their activities. Choose between the future perfect and future perfect progressive. Use the calendar to answer the questions.

AUGUST						
SUNDAY	MONDAY	TUESDAY	WEDNESDAY	THURSDAY	FRIDAY	SATURDAY
1 Aida walk 1/2 mi every day	**2** Arnie paint first bedroom	**3** Arnie paint second bedroom	**4** Arnie paint bathroom	**5** Aida start driving in carpool for day camp	**6**	**7**
8 Aida water garden daily	**9** Start picking vegetables daily	**10**	**11** Arnie paint downstairs →	**12**	**13**	**14**
15 Arnie finish painting indoors	**16** Arnie 4:00 P.M. dentist appointment	**17** Corrie pick blueberries for pies (need 3 quarts)	**18**	**19** Aida start baking pies for bake sale (agreed to bring 6 pies)	**20**	**21** Bake sale for fundraiser at Community Center
22 Aida start unpacking fall clothing →	**23**	**24**	**25** Iron and put away fall clothing	**26** Last day of carpool	**27**	**28**
29 Aida and Arnie pack for trip to Mom and Dad's	**30** →	**31** Travel to Mom and Dad's →				

1. (How many miles / Aida / walk / by August 31?)

    A: <u>How many miles will Aida have walked by August 31?</u>

    B: <u>She'll have walked 15½ miles.</u>

2. (How long / Aida / walk / by August 31?)

   A: _____

   B: _____

3. (How many rooms / Arnie / paint / by August 5?)

   A: _____

   B: _____

4. (How long / Arnie / paint downstairs / by August 15?)

   A: _____

   B: _____

5. (on August 16, / Arnie / leave / for his dentist appointment / by 4:00?)

   A: _____

   B: _____

6. (Aida / unpack / all the fall clothing / by August 23?)

   A: _____

   B: _____

7. (How long / Aida / drive in the carpool / by August 19?)

   A: _____

   B: _____

8. (How many quarts of blueberries / Corrie / pick / by August 19?)

   A: _____

   B: _____

9. (How many pies / Aida / bake / by August 21?)

   A: _____

   B: _____

10. (they / finish / packing for the trip / by August 31?)

    A: _____

    B: _____

UNIT 7

PART III Negative Questions and Tag Questions, Additions and Responses

Negative Yes/No Questions and Tag Questions

1 | AFFIRMATIVE AND NEGATIVE TAG QUESTIONS AND SHORT ANSWERS

Anne-Marie wants to rent an apartment. Complete her conversations with the landlord. Use appropriate tags. Write short answers based on the apartment ad.

> N. Smithfield unfurn. 1 BR in owner occup. bldg., renovated kitchen w. all new appliances, incl. DW, near all transp. & shopping, $500/mo. + util. Avail. for immed. occup. No pets. 555-7738

1. ANNE-MARIE: The rent is $500, _isn't it?_

    LANDLORD: _Yes, it is._

2. ANNE-MARIE: That includes electricity, _____

    LANDLORD: _____

3. ANNE-MARIE: The apartment isn't furnished, _____

    LANDLORD: _____

4. ANNE-MARIE: You've renovated the kitchen, _____

    LANDLORD: _____

5. ANNE-MARIE: The kitchen doesn't have a dishwasher, _____

    LANDLORD: _____

6. ANNE-MARIE: You just put in a new refrigerator, _____

    LANDLORD: _____

7. ANNE-MARIE: A bus stops nearby, _____

    LANDLORD: _____

8. ANNE-MARIE: I can't move in right away, _____

    LANDLORD: _____

9. **ANNE-MARIE:** You won't allow pets, _____

   LANDLORD: _____

10. **ANNE-MARIE:** You live right in the building, _____

    LANDLORD: _____

2 | NEGATIVE *YES/NO* QUESTIONS AND SHORT ANSWERS

*Todd and a realtor are discussing two communities—North Smithfield and Greenwood. Complete their conversation. Use negative **yes/no** questions to ask about Greenwood. Write short answers based on the information in the box.*

Greenwood—Community Profile

Greenwood became a town in 1782.
Schools: Greenwood High School, Greenwood Community College
Shopping: Greenwood Mall
Transportation: local public bus
Recreational Facilities: Briar State Park, Greenwood Beach (private), Davis Baseball Stadium (planned for next year)
Cultural Opportunities: movie theaters (Greenwood Mall)
Average Rent: $678

1. **REALTOR:** North Smithfield has a community college.

   TODD: *Doesn't Greenwood have a community college?*

   REALTOR: *Yes, it does.*

2. **REALTOR:** North Smithfield built a public beach.

   TODD: _____

   REALTOR: _____

3. **REALTOR:** There's an airport in North Smithfield.

   TODD: _____

   REALTOR: _____

4. **REALTOR:** You can see live theater performances in North Smithfield.

   TODD: _____

   REALTOR: _____

(continued)

5. REALTOR: People in North Smithfield shop at a nearby mall.

   TODD: _____

   REALTOR: _____

6. REALTOR: The average rent in North Smithfield is under $700.

   TODD: _____

   REALTOR: _____

7. REALTOR: North Smithfield has been a town for more than a hundred years.

   TODD: _____

   REALTOR: _____

8. REALTOR: They're going to build a baseball stadium in North Smithfield.

   TODD: _____

   REALTOR: _____

3 | NEGATIVE YES/NO QUESTIONS AND TAG QUESTIONS

*Complete the conversations. Use the correct form of the verbs in parentheses. Write negative **yes/no** questions and tag questions.*

A. Ari: ____*Didn't*____ you ____*move in*____ last week?
   1. (move in)

   Dan: Yes. You haven't been living here very long yourself, ____*have you*____?
   2.

   Ari: Oh, it's been about a year now.

   Dan: It's a nice place to live, _____?
   3.

   Ari: We think so.

B. Katie: You haven't seen the letter carrier this morning, _____?
   1.

   Dan: No. Why?

   Katie: I don't think our mail is being forwarded from our old address.

   Dan: _____ you _____ one of those
   2. (fill out)
   change-of-address forms?

   Katie: Yes. But that was almost a month ago. We should be getting our mail by now,

   _____?
   3.

   Dan: I would think so.

C. **Dan:** _____ there an all-night supermarket nearby?
       1. (be)

   Mia: Yes. It's at 10th and Walnut.

   Dan: I know where that is. _____ there _____ a restaurant there?
                                                2. (used to / be)

   Mia: That's right. It closed last year.

   Dan: That's strange. It hadn't been there very long, _____?
                                                              3.

   Mia: About a year. I guess the location just wasn't good for a restaurant.

D. **Ari:** The new neighbors are really friendly, _____?
                                                    1.

   Mia: Yes. That reminds me. The people across the hall invited us over for coffee and cake on Saturday afternoon. You haven't made any plans for then, _____?
                                                                                                                                                              2.

   Ari: Well, I was going to work on our taxes.

   Mia: _____ you _____ a little break?
                              3. (can / take)

   Ari: Sure. Why not?

4 | NEGATIVE YES/NO QUESTIONS AND TAG QUESTIONS

*The new tenants are going to visit their neighbors. They want to confirm some of the assumptions they have. Read their assumptions. Then write negative **yes/no** questions or tag questions. For some sentences, both types of questions are possible. (Remember: The only time you can use negative **yes/no** questions is when you think the answer is "Yes.")*

1. We think the people in Apartment 4F have lived here a long time.

   The people in Apartment 4F have lived here a long time, haven't they?

   OR

   Haven't the people in Apartment 4F lived here a long time?

2. I don't think our apartment had been occupied for a while.

   Our apartment hadn't been occupied for a while, had it?

3. We believe this is a good building.

   _____

4. It seems that the owner takes good care of it.

   _____

(continued)

5. It looks like he has just finished renovations on the lobby.

6. We don't think that he painted our apartment before we moved in.

7. I have the impression he doesn't talk very much.

8. I don't think the rent will increase next year.

9. It looks like some new people will be moving into Apartment 1B.

10. We have the impression that this is a really nice place to live.

UNIT 8

So, Too, Neither, Not either, and But

1 | AFFIRMATIVE AND NEGATIVE ADDITIONS

This is a true story about twin sisters. Complete the story with affirmative and negative additions.

A Birthday Surprise

Tamara Rabi and Adriana Scott are twin sisters who were born in Guadalajara, Mexico. However, the twins didn't meet until shortly after their 20th birthday.

Tamara and Adriana were adopted and grew up in different parts of New York. Adriana's adoptive mother knew that her daughter had a twin, __but__ Tamara's mother __didn't__. When Tamara began her studies at Hofstra University, a fellow student said that she looked really familiar, and _____ 3. did another and then another. At her 20th birthday party, one of the guests told her about his friend Adriana. Adriana was from Mexico, and Tamara was _____ 4. Adriana didn't know her birth parents, and _____ 5. did Tamara. Adriana's parents had adopted their child as an infant, and so _____ 6. Tamara's. The most surprising thing of all was that the two girls had the same birthday. Tamara was intrigued. She decided to contact Adriana by e-mail several days after the party.

(continued)

Adriana and Tamara found that they were not exactly alike. For example, Tamara likes Chinese food, _____ Adriana doesn't. Because she had worn braces,
7.
Adriana's teeth are straight, but Tamara's _____. Still, they share many
8.
similarities, and when they exchanged photographs, they couldn't believe how much they resembled each other. The twins agreed to meet.

On the day of their meeting, Tamara didn't want to go, and Adriana _____
9.
either. They were both afraid of what might happen next, but Adriana had invited friends to come along, _____ so had her sister. Having their friends there made them
10.
feel safe.

Shortly after their 20th birthday, the twins were reunited. Adriana received a wonderful gift, and her sister did _____: They received the gift of each other!
11.

2 | AFFIRMATIVE OR NEGATIVE?

Complete the conversations with affirmative and negative additions and responses.

A. **Kaleb:** I've heard that there's a twins festival every year.

   Karen: ___*So have*___ I.
   1.
   Kaleb: I didn't realize that there were enough twins around to have a festival.

   Karen: I _____. But hundreds of them attended the festival last year.
   2.
   Kaleb: I'm talking about the festival in Twinsburg, Ohio.

   Karen: I _____. Did you know that some of the people who go there actually
   3.
   fall in love and get married?

   Kaleb: Are you kidding?

   Karen: No. In 1998, Diane Sanders and her twin sister Darlene went to the festival in
   Twinsburg, and Craig Sanders and his brother Mark _____. Diane and
   4.
   Craig fell in love, and _____ Darlene and Mark.
   5.

Kaleb: Let me guess. Their children are twins.

Karen: Not exactly. Diane and Craig have identical twin sons, _____ Darlene and Mark _____. They have two singletons—one daughter was born in
6.
2001 and the other in 2003.

Kaleb: What's a singleton?

Karen: A child that isn't a twin.

B. **Ellie:** I thought I knew where the expression "Siamese twins" came from, _____ I _____. I had to look it up.
1.

Grant: What did you find out?

Ellie: Well, you know it refers to identical twins whose bodies are joined. Chang and Eng Bunker were conjoined twins who were born in Siam in 1811. The term was originally used to describe them. The preferred term today is "conjoined twins."

Grant: I remember reading about them. Most doctors at the time had never seen conjoined twins, and _____ anyone else. Chang and Eng became famous.
2.

Ellie: It's interesting. They ended up living in the United States. Chang got married, and _____ Eng. Their wives were sisters. Chang and his wife had 10
3.
children, and Eng and his wife had 11.

Grant: Do you know how they died?

Ellie: When they were older, Chang was sick, _____ Eng _____.
4.
He was still strong and healthy. One night Eng woke up, and his brother was dead. Eng died the same night.

C. **Kim:** More and more women in the United States are having children later in life.

Amy: Women in Europe _____. The average age of new mothers is rising
1.
there.

Kim: Because of the fact that new mothers are older and because of fertility treatments, the number of triplets, quadruplets, and quintuplets will continue to increase.

Amy: And _____ the number of twins.
2.

3 | AFFIRMATIVE OR NEGATIVE

Look at this information about twins festivals. Then complete the sentences about the festivals. Use the information in parentheses to write appropriate additions and responses.

Twins Festivals			
LOCATION	Twinsburg, Ohio, U.S.A	Pleucadeuc, France	Beijing, China
YEAR STARTED	1976	1994	2004
TIME OF YEAR	first week of August	mid-August	first week of October
WHO ATTENDS	twins, triplets, quads, quints, and their families	twins, triplets, quads, quints, and their families	twins and the general public
TYPES OF EVENTS	talent show, parade, contests, food, fireworks, photos	music, parade, photographs, food	entertainment, social events
COST	$15, additional costs for triplets, quads, and quints	free	free
REGISTRATION	recommended	recommended	none required

1. Twinsburg, Ohio, has a twins festival each year, __and so does Pleucadeuc, France OR and Pleucadeuc, France, does too__.
   (Pleucadeuc, France)
2. Twinsburg was holding its festival in the 1980s, _____.
   (Pleucadeuc)
3. Pleucadeuc doesn't charge an entrance fee, _____.
   (Beijing)
4. The Twinsburg festival isn't free, _____.
   (the Pleucadeuc and Beijing festivals)
5. Twinsburg will celebrate its festival next year, _____.
   (Pleucadeuc)
6. Twinsburg festival participants should register, _____.
   (participants at Pleucadeuc)
7. The Pleucadeuc festival doesn't have a talent show, _____.
   (the Beijing festival)
8. Twinsburg schedules its festival for August, _____.
   (Pleucadeuc)
9. Twins pay $15 at the Twinsburg festival, _____.
   (triplets, quads, and quints)
10. Pleucadeuc didn't sponsor a festival in 1990, _____.
    (Beijing)
11. Twins have gone to the Twinsburg festival for many years, _____.
    (their families)

PART IV Gerunds and Infinitives

Gerunds and Infinitives: Review and Expansion

UNIT 9

1 | GERUND OR INFINITIVE?

Complete these statements with the correct form—gerund or infinitive—of the verb **watch**. (Note: In some cases, both the infinitive and the gerund will be correct.)

1. The children wanted ____to watch____ television.
2. I suggest ____watching____ television.
3. We would like _____ television.
4. Do you need _____ television?
5. I was busy, so I really couldn't afford _____ television.
6. I should have stopped, but I continued _____ television.
7. Has a teacher ever encouraged you _____ television?
8. Some people dislike _____ television.
9. Others absolutely refuse _____ television.
10. Please turn off all the lights after you finish _____ television.
11. What time did you start _____ television?
12. My sister is addicted. She can't help _____ television.
13. How long ago did you quit _____ television?
14. Do you mind _____ television?
15. My roommate and I have decided _____ television.
16. I feel like _____ television.
17. They considered _____ television.
18. He keeps _____ television.
19. When you're tired, you seem _____ television.
20. Are they going to the movies or planning _____ television?

2 | GERUND OR INFINITIVE?

Use the correct form—gerund or infinitive—of the verbs in parentheses to complete this article.

TOO ANGRY __to remember__ THE COMMERCIALS?
1. (remember)

According to a new study, __watching__ violent TV shows makes it difficult __to recall__ brand names or commercial messages. Violence creates anger, and instead of __hearing__ the commercials, viewers are attempting __to calm__ themselves down after violent scenes. The conclusion: __Sponsoring__ violent programs may not be profitable for advertisers.

2. (watch)
3. (recall)
4. (hear)
5. (calm)
6. (Sponsor)

This conclusion is good news for the parents, teachers, and lawmakers who are struggling __to limit__ the amount of violence on U.S. television. They had a small victory in the late 1990s, when lawmakers and the television industry designed a TV-ratings system. Unfortunately, Congress did not ask parents __to participate__ in __creating__ the system, and the industry does not invite parents __to preview__ shows before it assigns ratings. As a result, parents are still guessing about the content of the shows their kids watch.

7. (limit)
8. (participate)
9. (create)
10. (preview)

Why are parents objecting to __having__ violence in television shows? The numbers tell the story: A typical child will see 8,000 murders and 100,000 acts of violence between the ages of 3 and 12! It's impossible __to believe__ that this input won't affect young children. In fact, researchers have noted the following possible effects of __viewing__ this much violence:

11. (have)
12. (believe)
13. (view)

1. Children may become less sensitive to other people's suffering.
2. They may also become fearful of __interacting__ with other people.
3. They may be more likely __to behave__ in a way that is harmful to others.

14. (interact)
15. (behave)

Gerunds and Infinitives: Review and Expansion | **45**

Studies have shown that a majority of people want commercial TV _____
16. (produce)
more educational and informational programs. In addition, more than 75 percent prefer
_____ the number of hours of TV that children watch, and the American
17. (limit)
Academy of Pediatrics recommends _____ children _____ more
18. (not permit)   19. (watch)
than one to two hours per day.

It's hard _____ why the entertainment industry resists _____
20. (understand)   21. (make)
changes. Parents, teachers, and doctors are urging the industry _____ clearer
22. (develop)
ratings and _____ violence in children's shows. What's more, violent TV
23. (get rid of)
shows don't seem _____ companies an effective way _____ their
24. (offer)   25. (advertise)
products. Even artists in the television business feel that it's time _____ the
26. (decrease)
amount of violence in American TV shows and have warned the industry executives
_____ _____ change.
27. (not continue) 28. (avoid)

The industry may choose _____ attention to the public, but it will not be
29. (not pay)
able to ignore Congress. Lawmakers want _____ the way networks market
30. (investigate)
violent shows to teenagers. They are also asking the industry _____ violence-
31. (schedule)
free hours, when no violent content is allowed. Hopefully, parents in the United States will
someday feel good about _____ the family TV.
32. (turn on)

3 | GERUND OR INFINITIVE?

A TV talk-show host is talking to a doctor about children and TV violence. Complete the interview with the appropriate word or phrase from the boxes plus the gerund or infinitive form of the verb in parentheses.

| fed up with | likely | ~~shocked~~ | unwilling | used to |

HOST: I was ___shocked to learn___ that children will see 100,000 acts of violence on
              1. (learn)
television before they are 12. I had no idea it was that bad. It also appears that the
networks are _____. They seem pretty satisfied with things the
                  2. (change)
way they are.

(continued)

DOCTOR: Yes, I think that they're _____ all the responsibility on the
3. (put)

viewer. That's the way it's always been, and they're accustomed to it.

HOST: The networks may not want to change, but I know a lot of us are really very

_____ violence during family viewing times. We're really sick of
4. (see)

it. A lot of my friends don't even turn on the cartoons anymore.

DOCTOR: That's probably a good idea. Several studies show that children are more

_____ others after they watch violent cartoons. It's really quite
5. (hit)

predictable.

| decide | dislike | force | hesitate | stop |

HOST: OK. Now what can we do about this problem?

DOCTOR: Well, viewers can make a big difference. First of all, we have to put a lot of pressure on

the networks and _____ them _____ shows more clearly.
6. (rate)

They'll give in if enough viewers tell them they must.

HOST: What else?

DOCTOR: When you see something you don't like, pick up the phone immediately. Don't wait. We

shouldn't _____ the networks about material that we find
7. (tell)

offensive. Recently a network _____ a violent ad for another
8. (run)

show right in the middle of a family sitcom. So many people complained that they

reversed that decision and _____ the ad in that time slot.
9. (show)

HOST: Violence bothers my kids, but they _____ a show once it starts.
10. (turn off)

They want to stick it out to the end.

| consider | forbid | insist on | permit |

DOCTOR: Parents have to assert their authority and _____ the channel
11. (change)

when violence appears. Sometimes they'll face a lot of resistance, but they should

be firm.

Gerunds and Infinitives: Review and Expansion | 47

HOST: You know, in a lot of families, parents work until six. They can't successfully _____ their children _____ certain
12. (turn on)
shows. They're just not around to enforce the rules.

DOCTOR: There's help from the electronics industry in the form of a V-chip.

HOST: What exactly is a V-chip?

DOCTOR: It's a chip built into television sets. The V-chip doesn't _____
children _____ violent shows. It blocks them electronically.
13. (tune in)

HOST: It sounds like something all parents should _____.
14. (own)

| advise | agree | hesitate | keep |

HOST: Is there anything else that you _____ parents _____?
15. (do)

DOCTOR: Parents must _____ with their children. They shouldn't
16. (communicate)
_____ their kids about their feelings and opinions—and
17. (ask)
especially about their activities.

HOST: Thank you, Doctor, for _____ to us today.
18. (speak)

4 | OBJECTS WITH GERUNDS AND INFINITIVES

Read the conversations about watching television. Then use the correct forms of the words in parentheses to write summaries.

1. KIDS: Can we watch TV now?

   MOM: I'm sorry, but you have to finish your homework first.

   SUMMARY: _____Their mother didn't allow them to watch TV._____
   (their mother / allow / they / watch TV)

2. ANNIE: My parents finally bought me a new TV, but it has a V-chip.

   BEA: What's that?

   ANNIE: It's something that blocks violent shows so that I can't watch them.

   SUMMARY: _____
   (a V-chip / interfere with / Annie / watch violent shows)

(continued)

3. **Roger:** Our kids really seem to like *Reading Rainbow*.

   Cora: I know. It's so great that there's a high-quality TV show about reading and learning.

   SUMMARY: _____
   (*Reading Rainbow* / encourage / they / get interested in books)

4. **Dad:** You were having some pretty bad nightmares last night, Jennifer. I think you'd better stop watching those cop shows.

   Jennifer: OK, but I really love them.

   SUMMARY: _____
   (her father / tell / Jennifer / watch cop shows / anymore)

5. **Students:** We want to watch the TV news, but the reporting on adult news shows is usually really frightening.

   Teacher: Try *Nick News with Linda Ellerbee*. It's a great news show for kids.

   SUMMARY: _____
   (the teacher / recommend / they / watch *Nick News*)

6. **Sue:** I'll never forget that great Knicks game we watched last year.

   Bob: What Knicks game?

   Sue: Don't you remember? We saw it together! The Knicks beat the Rockets 91–85.

   SUMMARY: _____
   (Bob / remember / they / see that game)

7. **Fred:** Does Sharif still watch *Z-Men* every Saturday?

   Abu: No. We explained that it was too violent for him, and he decided not to watch it anymore.

   SUMMARY: _____
   (Sharif's parents / persuade / he / watch *Z-Men*)

8. **Mom:** Sara, it's nine o'clock. Time to turn off the TV.

   Sara: Oh, Mom. Just a little longer, OK?

   Mom: You know the rules. No TV after nine o'clock.

   SUMMARY: _____
   (the mother / insist on / Sara / turn off the TV)

9. **Aziza:** This is boring. What's on the other channels?

   Ben: I don't know. Where's the remote control?

   SUMMARY: _____
   (Aziza / want / Ben / change the channel)

10. **Nick:** *Primer Impacto*, my favorite TV news program, starts in five minutes.

    Paul: I've never understood why you watch that show. It's in Spanish, and you don't speak Spanish at all.

    SUMMARY: _____
    (Nick / can't get used to / Paul / watch a Spanish-language news program)

5 | EDITING

Read this student's essay. There are eleven mistakes in the use of the gerund and infinitive. The first mistake is already corrected. Find and correct ten more.

Asoka Jayawardena
English 220
May 30

Violence on TV

I'm tired of ~~hear~~ *hearing* that violence on TV causes violence at home, in school, and on the streets. Almost all young people watch TV, but not all of them are involved in committing crimes! In fact, very few people choose acting in violent ways. To watch TV, therefore, is not the cause.

Groups like the American Medical Society should stop making a point of to tell people what to watch. If we want living in a free society, it is necessary having freedom of choice. Children need learn values from their parents. It should be the parents' responsibility deciding what their child can or cannot watch. The government and other interest groups should avoid to interfere in these personal decisions. Limiting our freedom of choice is not the answer. If parents teach their children respecting life, children can enjoy to watch TV without any negative effects.

UNIT 10 Make, Have, Let, Help, and Get

1 | CONTRAST: MAKE, HAVE, LET, HELP, AND GET

Complete this article about the roles that animals can play in our lives. Circle the correct verbs.

The Animal-Human Connection

Can pets get / (help) humans lead better lives? Not only animal lovers but also some
       1.
health-care professionals believe that pets let / get us improve our quality of everyday living.
                                                2.
   Pets have / help their owners stay healthy. For example, dogs need daily exercise, and
        3.
this has / makes many owners turn off their television sets or computers and go outside for
     4.
a walk. While walking their dogs, they receive the health benefits of being physically active,
and they are able to talk to the people they see on the street or in the park. These positive
human relationships get / make dog owners feel happy, which can lead to longer, healthier
                     5.
lives. Speaking of positive relationships, it is interesting to note that research shows pet
owners often have lower blood pressure as a result of spending time with their animals. It
seems that pets get / make their owners to relax.
              6.
   Animals can also play an important role for humans who are sick. In some cases,
health-care professionals let / have animals provide
                         7.
attention, affection, and companionship for their patients.
The animals don't replace other forms of medical care,
but they help / have patients recover more quickly and live
         8.
longer. The Delta Society is a nonprofit organization that

50

promotes the idea of using animals in places such as hospitals, nursing homes, and rehabilitation centers. The society lets / gets volunteers to work with those in need, but it doesn't let / make just any pet participate in its programs. It makes / gets pets and their
9.   10.   11.
owners complete training courses so that the animals will be friendly and give comfort to the humans they meet.

In addition to helping those who are ill, animals can assist people with disabilities. Guide dogs help / make people who are blind cross busy streets or take public
12.
transportation. People who are unable to move their arms or legs can help / have their dogs
13.
open doors, turn lights off and on, and even answer the telephone. Special hearing dogs make / let hearing-impaired owners pay attention when the doorbell rings, their baby cries,
14.
or a fire alarm sounds.

2 | MAKE, HAVE, LET, GET, AND HELP + OBJECT + CORRECT FORM OF THE VERB

Read this tip sheet from an animal welfare agency. Complete the sentences by adding pronoun objects and the correct form of the verbs in parentheses.

Dogs Are Family Members, Too

Whether your family has a dog or you'd like to bring a dog into your home, here are some things to consider.

If you're thinking about getting a dog . . .

- It takes time and money to care for a dog. Be sure that you have enough of both. A dog could be a member of your family for 15 years or more.

- Talking to everyone in your family will make _____*them feel*_____ part of the decision-
1. (feel)
making process, and they'll be more likely to welcome a dog as a new member of the family.

- Pets are not always welcome. Find out if your landlord will let _____ a dog
2. (keep)
in your apartment.

(continued)

- There are always animals available for adoption. Before buying a dog from a pet shop or a breeder, contact your local animal shelter. At the shelter, ask about classes or an adoption program that will help _____ what kind of dog is best for you and your family. Also talk to staff
  3. (decide)
  members about the health and history of a dog that you want to adopt. It's a good idea to have _____ you as much information as possible.
  4. (give)

If there are children in the family . . .

- Your child may really want a dog, and she may promise to take care of your family's new pet, but honestly, it may be impossible to get _____ it. Consider dividing pet care
  5. (do)
  responsibilities among all members of the family, including children. Depending on the children's ages, it's certainly possible to have _____ specific tasks such as taking the dog
  6. (take care of)
  for a walk after school or giving the dog food and water.

- Children may have to learn to be gentle. Get _____ animals need respect
  7. (realize)
  just like humans, and that means no hitting, kicking, riding, or pulling the tail of the family dog.

- At some point, your dog will get overexcited when he is playing. Children should know what to do to get _____.
  8. (calm down)

- It pays to be careful. If you have a very young child, she may love the family pet, but never let _____ with the family dog alone. Adult supervision is essential.
  9. (play)

If there is a new baby coming into the family . . .

- Your dog will know that there's been a change, and he will probably be excited, anxious, and curious. It's up to you to help _____. Before the baby arrives, introduce
  10. (adjust)
  him to baby sounds. He should also get accustomed to seeing a baby, so use a doll or let _____ time around a real infant if possible.
  11. (spend)

- Your dog may need training so that you can get _____ you at all times
  12. (obey)
  when he is around the new baby.

- Although you'll be busy with your new baby, spending time with your dog will make _____ that he is still an important member of the family. It will also help
  13. (understand)
  _____ during this very busy time in your life.
  14. (relax)

If you want to know more, contact our organization and let _____ you with
  15. (provide)
more detailed information on dogs and families.

3 | AFFIRMATIVE AND NEGATIVE STATEMENTS

Read the conversations. Then use the correct forms of the verbs in parentheses to complete the summaries. Add pronouns when necessary.

1. JOHN: Mom, can I get a horse?

    MOTHER: No, of course you can't get a horse!

    SUMMARY: John's mother _____*didn't let him get a horse.*_____
    (let)

2. MOTHER: Instead of a horse, will you agree to adopt a dog or a cat?

    JOHN: OK.

    SUMMARY: John's mother _____
    (get)

3. MOTHER: You can make the choice.

    JOHN: I'd rather have a cat.

    SUMMARY: His mother _____
    (let)

4. MOTHER: Now, you have to do some research on pet care.

    JOHN: I can do that. I know a couple of animal-protection groups that have good information on their websites.

    SUMMARY: She _____
    (make)

5. JOHN: Do I have to do all of the research by myself?

    MOTHER: Yes, you do.

    SUMMARY: John's mother _____
    (help)

6. JOHN: I found out that I have to be 18 to adopt a pet. Can you fill out and sign the adoption application forms for me?

    MOTHER: Sure.

    SUMMARY: John _____
    (get)

7. MOTHER: First, you have to explain the adoption process to me.

    JOHN: I have all of the information right here.

    SUMMARY: John's mother _____
    (have)

8. JOHN: I have enough money to pay the adoption fees.

    MOTHER: You may need the money later. I'll pay the fees.

    SUMMARY: John's mother _____
    (make)

4 | EDITING

Read this university student's e-mail. She made seven mistakes in the use of **make**, **have**, **let**, **help**, *and* **get**. *The first mistake is already corrected. Find and correct six more.*

Hi, Ami!

Thanks for staying in touch. Your e-mails always make me ~~to smile~~ *smile*—even when I'm feeling stressed. Knowing that I have a good friend like you really helps me relax and not take things so seriously. My classes are difficult this semester. I still can't believe that three of my professors are making them write 20-page papers.

At the end of last semester, my roommates and I decided to get a dog. Actually, my roommates made the decision and then got me go along with it. I made them promise to take care of the dog, but guess who's doing most of the work! Don't misunderstand me. I love Ellie and appreciate what a great companion she is. I take her for a walk every morning and every night and make her run and play in the park near our apartment as often as I can because I know how much she enjoys it. Still, I wish I could have my roommates to spend just an hour a week with "our" dog. At this point, I can't even get them feeding Ellie, and now they want to move to an apartment complex that won't let us to have a dog. I think I'm going to have to choose whether to live with my roommates or with Ellie—and I think I'm going to choose Ellie!

Take care. I'll write again soon.

Neha

PART V Phrasal Verbs

Phrasal Verbs: Review

UNIT 11

1 | PARTICLES

Complete the phrasal verbs with particles from the box. You will use some particles more than once.

ahead	back	down	off
on	out	over	up

Phrasal Verb   **Meaning**

1. catch ___on___   become popular
2. cheer _____   make someone feel happier
3. do _____   do again
4. get _____   make progress, succeed
5. let _____   allow to leave
6. let _____   disappoint
7. look _____   examine
8. pick _____   select or identify
9. take _____   return
10. try _____   use to find out if it works
11. turn _____   raise the volume
12. turn _____   lower the volume
13. use _____   consume
14. write _____   write on a piece of paper
15. put _____   delay
16. think _____   invent

55

2 | PHRASAL VERBS

Read about New Year traditions around the world. Complete the article with the correct forms of the phrasal verbs in the box. Choose the verbs that are closest in meaning to the words in parentheses.

| burn up | cut down | get together | give out | go back | go out |
| ~~pay back~~ | put on | put together | set up | throw away | |

Starting New

Wearing new clothes, __paying back__ **1. (repay)** debts, lighting candles—many cultures share similar New Year traditions. In Iran, for example, people celebrate *Now Ruz*, or New Day, on the first day of spring. A few days before the festival, families _____ bushes and _____ piles of wood. They
2. (bring down by cutting) ... **3. (assemble)**
set the piles on fire, and before the wood _____, each family
4. (burn completely)
member jumps over one of the fires and says, "I give you my pale face, and I take your red one." The day before the New Year begins, the family _____ a table
5. (prepare for use)
in the main room with special foods and objects, such as colored eggs, cake, and the *haft-sin*, seven objects with names beginning with the sound "s." Everyone _____
6. (cover the body with)
new clothes, and the family _____ around the table. When the New
7. (meet)
Year begins, family members hug each other and _____ gifts,
8. (distribute)
especially to the children. For the next 12 days, people visit each other, but on the 13th day, it is unlucky to be inside a house, so people _____ and spend the day
9. (leave)
in parks and fields, where they have picnics, listen to music, and play sports. They don't _____ home until sunset. At the end of the day, everyone
10. (return)
"_____" bad luck by throwing wheat or lentils into a river.
11. (discard)

3 | PHRASAL VERBS AND OBJECTS

Complete the conversations with the phrasal verbs and objects in parentheses. Place the object between the verb and the participle when possible.

A. **Vijay:** We need about two dozen candles for *Diwali*.

   Nira: I'll _____*pick them up*_____ after work.
   1. (pick up / them)

   Vijay: While you're there, why don't you get some new decorations?

   Nira: Let's have the children _____. You know how
   2. (pick out / them)
   excited they get about the Hindu New Year.

B. **Eva:** Why do you _____
   1. (empty out / the money and everything else in your pockets)
   on *Rosh Hashana*?

   Simon: It's a custom for the Jewish New Year to throw what's in our pockets into moving water. It's like getting rid of last year's bad memories.

   Eva: Here's my cigarette lighter. I'd love to _____.
   2. (throw away / it)

C. **May:** When will we _____ for the Chinese New Year?
   1. (set off / the firecrackers)

   Ning: Not until dark.

   May: Don't the firecrackers have something to do with evil spirits?

   Ning: Yes. We believe that the noise _____.
   2. (keep away / them)

D. **Liam:** Are you decorating for Christmas?

   Zoé: No, we're _____ for Kwanzaa, the African-American
   1. (hang up / these streamers)
   harvest celebration. It comes at the same time as Christmas and New Year.

   Liam: What is your mom putting on the table?

   Zoé: That's a *kinara*. We _____ to hold the Kwanzaa candles.
   2. (set up / it)

E. **Kelsey:** Do you usually make New Year's resolutions?

   Ian: Yes, and I _____
   1. (write down / all of the resolutions that I make each year)
   because they're so easy to forget by February.

   Kelsey: This year I'd like to stop eating desserts.

   Ian: I _____ for a few months last year. I lost five pounds.
   2. (gave up / them)

4 | EDITING

Read this person's list of New Year's resolutions. There are eleven mistakes in the use of phrasal verbs. The first mistake is already corrected. Find and correct ten more.

New Year's Resolutions

Wake ~~out~~ **up** earlier. (No later than 7:30!)
Work out at the gym at least 3 times a week.
Lose 5 pounds. (Give over eating so many desserts.)

Be more conscious of the environment:
— Don't throw down newspapers. Recycle them.
— Save energy. Turn on the lights when I leave the apartment.

Straighten up my room:
— Hang out my clothes when I take off them.
— Put my books back where they belong.
— Give some of my old books and clothing that I no longer wear away.

Don't put off doing my homework assignments. Hand in them on time!

Read more.

Use the dictionary more. (Look over words I don't know.)

When someone calls and leaves a message, call them back right away. Don't put off it!

Get to know my neighbors. Ask them for coffee over.

UNIT 12
Phrasal Verbs: Separable and Inseparable

1 | PARTICLES

Complete the phrasal verbs with the correct particles.

Phrasal Verb	Meaning
1. call ____back____	return a phone call
2. get _____	recover from an illness or a bad situation
3. cross _____	draw a line through
4. call _____	cancel
5. drop _____	visit unexpectedly
6. look _____	be careful
7. keep _____	continue
8. talk _____	persuade
9. blow _____	explode
10. turn _____	reject
11. run _____	meet accidentally
12. put _____	return to its original place
13. work _____	solve
14. go _____	continue
15. find _____	discover
16. turn _____	lower the volume

2 | PHRASAL VERBS

Complete these paragraphs with the appropriate form of the phrasal verbs from the boxes.

catch on	~~come out~~	figure out	go off	help out
take away	team up with	turn off	turn on	

A. There have been a lot of changes since the first consumer cell phones __came out__ (1.) in the 1980s. The original phones were big, heavy, and very expensive. After designers _____ (2.) how to make them smaller and more affordable, they really began to _____ (3.). Now, people all over the world are _____ (4.) their mobile phones and using them in ways that could never have been imagined in the 1980s. Several years ago, wireless companies _____ (5.) digital-photography experts to produce camera phones, which are now popular with consumers. Internet access is another way that cell phones _____ us _____ (6.) by keeping us connected and informed. However, there is a negative side to wireless technology. For example, when cell phones _____ (7.) in restaurants, movie theaters, and classrooms, they can be annoying. When we're forced to listen to other people's conversations in public places, it _____ (8.) our privacy and the privacy of the person talking on the phone. Clearly, it's sometimes best to _____ our cell phones _____ (9.).

end up	find out	keep up with	look over
pick out	put away	use up	watch out for

B. Cell phones let us _____ friends and family whenever and wherever

   we want, but they can _____ being very expensive. It's great to stay

   in touch, but it's hard to know when to stop talking and _____ our

   mobile phones _____. Cell phone companies advertise reasonably

   priced calling packages, but it's easy to _____ all the minutes on a

   basic plan. Many of us have _____ the hard way what it's like to pay

   overage charges. Smart consumers do comparison shopping and _____

   wireless service with features such as free weekend and evening minutes, unlimited calls to

   family members, and no roaming charges when customers go out of their calling area. Smart

   consumers also _____ their cell phone contract carefully before they

   sign it. They realize how important it is to _____ hidden fees.

3 | PHRASAL VERBS AND OBJECT PRONOUNS

Complete the conversations. Use phrasal verbs and pronouns.

1. **Luis:** I thought you were going to ask the Riveras over for dinner.

   Ines: I did. I ___asked them over___ for Friday night.

2. **Luis:** Did you invite their son too? He gets along well with Jimmy.

   Ines: That's a good idea. He really does _____.

3. **Ines:** If you run into Marta tomorrow, invite her too. She knows the Riveras.

   Luis: I usually don't _____ on Tuesdays. If we want her to come,

   we should call.

4. **Ines:** I'd like you to straighten up your room before the Riveras come over.

   Jimmy: No problem. I'll _____ as soon as I come home from school

   Friday.

(continued)

62 | UNIT 12

5. **JIMMY:** There's a big game on TV at eight o'clock on Friday that I'd like to watch. Do we really have to get together with the Riveras on Friday?

   INES: Yes, we do. We haven't _____ since last summer. Besides, we canceled our dinner plans last month, and I don't want to cancel again.

6. **INES:** Maybe you could pick out some CDs to play during dinner.

   JIMMY: Sure. I'll _____ right now.

7. **INES:** I hope we can count on the Riveras to bring the dessert.

   LUIS: Don't worry. You can _____. If they promised to bring dessert, then they'll bring it.

8. **INES:** You can bring out the roast now. It's done.

   LUIS: Great. I'll _____ right away so we can eat. It smells great.

9. **INES:** Be careful! Don't pick up the pan without pot holders! It's hot!

   LUIS: Ow! Too late! I just _____.

10. **LUIS:** I'm going to turn down the music. It's a little too loud.

    INES: Oh, don't get up. I'll _____.

11. **LUIS:** Should I cover up the leftovers?

    INES: Uh-huh. Here's some aluminum foil. After you _____, you can put them in the refrigerator.

12. **INES:** You didn't eat much at dinner tonight. You're really sticking to your diet, aren't you?

    LUIS: That's right. I've _____ for three weeks now, and I plan to continue until I lose 15 pounds.

13. **INES:** Could you help me put away these folding chairs?

    LUIS: Why don't you rest? I'll _____.

14. **INES:** Don't forget to turn on the dishwasher before you go to bed.

    LUIS: I'll _____ now. That way I won't forget.

15. **INES:** Good night. I'm going to bed and try to figure out that crossword puzzle that's been giving me trouble.

    LUIS: Good luck! Let me know when you _____.

4 | DEFINITIONS

See if you can figure out this puzzle.

Across
- 4. Gets off (the bus)
- 7. Want
- 11. Mix up
- 13. Figure out
- 16. Opposite of *fall*
- 17. Leave out
- 18. Think up
- 19. These can run out of ink.
- 21. _____ it rains, it pours.
- 23. Call up
- 25. Don't go away. Please _____.
- 26. Street *(abbreviation)*
- 27. Middle
- 31. Call off
- 32. Indefinite article
- 33. Professional *(short form)*
- 34. Medical doctor *(abbreviation)*
- 36. What time _____ she usually show up?
- 38. Negative word
- 40. Take place
- 41. Put up (a building)

Down
- 1. Pick _____ up at 5:00. I'll be ready then.
- 2. Hello
- 3. You and I
- 4. Pick up
- 5. Advertisements *(short form)*
- 6. Hands in
- 7. Talk over
- 8. Tell off
- 9. Take back
- 10. Carry on
- 12. Look over
- 14. *am, is,* _____
- 15. Eastern Standard Time *(abbreviation)*
- 18. Drop _____ on
- 19. Put off
- 20. Come in
- 21. The music is loud. Please turn _____ down.
- 22. Pass out
- 24. Blow up
- 27. Her book _____ out last year.
- 28. Marcia always _____ up with more work than anyone else.
- 29. Rte. *(full word)*
- 30. *Drop in* means "to _____ unexpectedly."
- 31. You put a small bandage on it.
- 35. Don't guess. Look it _____.
- 37. Please go _____. Don't stop.
- 39. Either . . . _____

UNIT 13

PART **VI** Adjective Clauses

Adjective Clauses with Subject Relative Pronouns

1 | RELATIVE PRONOUNS

In many countries, people sometimes try to meet others through personal ads in magazines and newspapers. Circle the correct relative pronouns to complete these ads.

Best Friends—I'm a 28-year-old man (who)/ which enjoys reading, baseball, movies, and long
                                           1.
walks in the country. You're a 20-to-30-year-old woman who / whose interests are compatible with
                                                          2.
mine and who / whose believes that friendship is the basis of a good marriage. **7932**
         3.

Starstruck—You remind me of Johnny Depp, who / that is my favorite actor. I remind you of a
                                              4.
movie who / that is fun and full of surprises. Won't you be my leading man as we dance across the
      5.
screen of life? **3234**

Where Are You?—35-year-old career-oriented female that / which relaxes at the gym and
                                                      6.
who / whose personality varies from philosophical to funny seeks male counterpart. **9534**
7.

Forever—Are you looking for a relationship who / that will stand the test of time? Call this 28-year-
                                               8.
old male who / which believes in forever. **2312**
         9.

Soul Mates?—The things that / who make me happy are chocolate cake, travel, animals, music,
                             10.
and someone whose / who ideas of a good time are similar to mine. **1294**
            11.

Enough Said—I want to meet a guy who / whose is smart enough to read, active enough to run
                                      12.
for a bus that / who just left the stop, silly enough to appreciate Adam Sandler, and mature enough
        13.
to want a commitment. I'm a 25-year-old female who / which finds meaning in building a
                                                 14.
relationship and then a family. **6533**

2 | SUBJECT-VERB AGREEMENT

Read the results of a study about the ingredients of a happy marriage. Complete the information with appropriate relative pronouns and the correct form of the verbs in parentheses.

What It Takes to Have a Happy Marriage

ABILITY TO CHANGE AND ACCEPT CHANGE

Successful couples are those __who__ (1.) __are__ (2. be) able to adapt to changes __that/which__ (3.) __occur__ (4. occur) within the marriage or in the other partner. People __who__ (5.) __stay__ (6. stay) happily married see themselves "as free agents __who/that__ (7.) __make__ (8. make) choices in life."

ABILITY TO LIVE WITH THE UNCHANGEABLE

They can live with situations __that/which__ (9.) __do not change__ (10. not change). They accept the knowledge that there are some conflicts __that/which__ (11.) __remain__ (12. remain) unsolvable. This attitude relates to life in general. According to the study, people __whose__ (13.) marriages __come__ (14. come) to an end because of a crisis such as an illness or job loss tend to be individuals __who/that__ (15.) __are__ (16. be) unable to deal with the realities of life. Their only answer is to end the relationship.

ASSUMPTION OF "FOREVER"

Most newlyweds believe their marriage is "forever." This is an important belief __that/which__ (17.) __helps__ (18. help) the relationship survive problems.

TRUST

In marriage, trust allows for the sense of security __that/which__ (19.) __makes__ (20. make) long and satisfying relationships possible. It is the glue __that/which__ (21.) __holds__ (22. hold) the marriage together.

(continued)

ENJOYING EACH OTHER'S COMPANY

According to the study, "Although they may spend evenings quietly together in a room, the silence _____ _____ them is the comfortable silence of two
   23.   24. (surround)

people _____ _____ they do not have to talk to feel "close."
      25.   26. (know)

They can simply enjoy being together.

SHARED HISTORY

A marriage is a relationship _____ _____ a reality and history of
                              27.   28. (have)

its own. People in good marriages value their shared history and gain strength from it. They keep it alive with family stories and photos.

LUCK

What role does luck play? You need luck in choosing a partner _____
                                                                29.

_____ the ability to change and trust and love. You need luck, too, in the type
30. (have)

of family you come from. Research suggests that families _____ members
                                                            31.

_____ warm and supportive provide good preparation for future relationships.
32. (be)

You also need luck with life itself. This is often a question of attitude. According to the study,

"Couples _____ _____ themselves lucky are the ones
          33.   34. (consider)

_____ _____ luck where they are able to." They don't wait for
35.   36. (seize)

luck to come to them.

3 | SENTENCE COMBINING

Combine the pairs of sentences. Make the second sentence in each pair an adjective clause. Make any other necessary changes.

1. I met Rebecca in 1994. Rebecca is now my wife.

   I met Rebecca, who is now my wife, in 1994.

2. She was visiting her favorite aunt. Her aunt's apartment was right across from mine.

   _____

3. I was immediately attracted to Rebecca because of her smile. The smile was full of warmth and good humor.

   _____

4. I could see that Rebecca was a terrific woman. Her interests were similar to mine.

5. Ballroom dancing was one of our favorite activities. Ballroom dancing was very popular in those days.

6. We also enjoyed playing cards with some of our close friends. Our friends lived in the neighborhood.

7. Our friend Mike taught us how to ski. Mike was a professional skier.

8. We got married in a ski lodge. The ski lodge was in Vermont.

9. Our marriage has grown through the years. Our marriage means a lot to us both.

10. The love and companionship have gotten stronger. The love and companionship make us very happy.

11. Even the bad things have brought us closer together. Bad things have happened.

12. I really love Rebecca. Rebecca is not only my wife but also my best friend.

UNIT 14 Adjective Clauses with Object Relative Pronouns or *When* and *Where*

1 | RELATIVE PRONOUNS AND *WHEN* AND *WHERE*: SUBJECT AND OBJECT

Circle the correct words to complete these book dedications and acknowledgments.

A.

To my family, (which) / that has given me my first world, and to my friends, who / whom have
                    1.   **2.**

taught me how to appreciate the New World after all.

(Eva Hoffman, *Lost in Translation: A Life in a New Language.* New York: Penguin, 1989.)

B.

I'd like to thank everyone which / who has been in my life. But since I can't, I'll single out a few
                                  1.

who / whose were particularly helpful to me in the writing of this book . . . thanks to my loving and
2.

amazingly patient wife, Dianne, to all our friends whom / which we couldn't see while I was mired
                                                             2.

in self-examination, and to my family.

(Ben Fong-Torres, *The Rice Room.* New York: Hyperion, 1994.)

C.

My book would not have been written without the encouragement and collaboration of many people. I should like to thank my wife, who / that has seen little of me at home
                                                                    1.

during the last few years, for her understanding. . . . I should like to thank the NASA personnel at Houston, Cape Kennedy, and Huntsville, which / who showed me around
                                                                                 2.

their magnificent scientific and technical research centers . . . all the countless men and women around the globe whose / whom practical help, encouragement, and
                                                  3.

conversation made this book possible.

(Erich Von Däniken, *Chariots of the Gods?* New York: G.P. Putnam, 1977.)

D.

I ask the indulgence of the children <u>who / whose</u> may read this book for dedicating it to a
                                         1.
grown-up. I have a serious reason: he is the best friend I have in the world. I have another reason: this grown-up understands everything, even books about children. I have a third reason: he lives in France, <u>which / where</u> he is hungry and cold. He needs cheering up. If all
                                          2.
these reasons are not enough, I will dedicate this book to the child from <u>whom / who</u> this
                                                                              3.
grown-up grew. All grown-ups were once children—although few of them remember it.

(Antoine de Saint-Exupéry, *The Little Prince*. New York: Harcourt Brace, 1943.)

E.

The field-work on <u>which / that</u> this book is based covers a span of fourteen years, 1925–1939; the
                        1.
thinking covers the whole of my professional life, 1923–1948. . . . It is impossible to make articulate . . . the debt I owe to those hundreds of people of the Pacific Islands <u>who / whose</u> patience, tolerance of
                                                                                    2.
differences, faith in my goodwill, and eager curiosity made these studies possible. Many of the children <u>whom / which</u> I held in my arms and from <u>whom / whose</u> tense or relaxed behavior I learned lessons
   3.   **4.**
<u>who / that</u> could have been learned in no other way are now grown men and women; the life they live in
   5.
the records of an anthropologist must always have about it a quality of wonder both to the anthropologist and to themselves. . . .

(Margaret Mead, *Male and Female*. New York: William Morrow, 1949.)

F.

Nearly every person interviewed for this book has been given relevant portions of the manuscript to check for errors, but any mistakes remain my responsibility. Conversations and events <u>who / that</u> I did not hear or see have been reported as the participants remembered
         1.
them. . . . Much has been written about the decline of American education. It is a joy to describe one place <u>where / when</u> that shaky institution has experienced an unmistakable
                         2.
revival. . . . I hope this book will impart some of that excitement to any <u>which / who</u> wish to
                                                                               3.
set forth in the same direction as Jaime Escalante and the many other teachers in America like him.

(Jay Mathews, *Escalante: The Best Teacher in America*. New York: Henry Holt, 1988.)

(continued)

G.

... some contributions to my work come from people I have never met and probably never will. I am grateful ... to the citizens of the city of Portland and the county of Multnomah, Oregon, **which / whose**_{1.} taxes support the Multnomah County Library, without **whom / whose**_{2.} reference material this book would not have been written. I am also grateful to the archaeologists, anthropologists, and other specialists **who / whom**_{3.} wrote the books from **which / that**_{4.} I gathered most of this information for the setting and background of this novel. ... There are many who helped more directly ... Karen Auel, **that / who**_{5.} encouraged her mother more than she ever knew ... Cathy Humble, of **which / whom**_{6.} I asked the greatest favor one can ask of a friend—honest criticism—because I valued her sense of words.

(Jean M. Auel, *The Clan of the Cave Bear*. New York: Crown, 1980.)

2 | RELATIVE PRONOUNS AND *WHEN* AND *WHERE*: OBJECT

Read this article about book dedications and acknowledgments. Complete the information with **who(m)**, **which**, **that**, **whose**, **when**, or **where**, and the correct forms of the verbs in parentheses.

To L. F., without _____whose_____ *encouragement . . .*
1.

Dedication and acknowledgment pages are the places _____ an author
                                                          2.
_____ the people _____ support and assistance he or she
3. (thank)   4.
_____ valuable while writing. These words of gratitude are probably the last
5. (find)
ones _____ the author _____ for a book, but they'll be the
      6.   7. (write)
first ones _____ a reader _____. This fact may explain some
           8.   9. (read)
of the problems _____ writers _____ when writing these
                 10.   11. (face)
pages. The thanks should be gracious and well written, but the task of writing them most often comes at the end of a long project—a time _____ an author sometimes
                                                                         12.
_____ words. In the 16th and 17th centuries, _____ rich
13. (run out of)   14.
nobles _____ artists, writers were paid well for writing dedications in
        15. (support)
_____ they _____ their wealthy employers. Some "authors"
16.   17. (praise)
made a profession of dedication writing. They traveled the countryside with fake books into
_____ they _____ a new dedication at each rich family's house.
18.   19. (insert)

A modern writer usually dedicates a book to a family member, friend, or colleague with _____20._____ he or she _____21. (feel)_____ deeply connected. The dedication page is short and often contains only the initials of the person to _____22._____ the author _____23. (dedicate)_____ the work. In the acknowledgments, _____24._____ the author _____25. (have)_____ more room, everyone from reference librarians to proofreaders is thanked.

Unfortunately, most writers' handbooks give authors very little help with dedications and acknowledgments. "It's just something _____26._____ you _____27. (be supposed to)_____ know how to handle," complains one author.

3 | RELATIVE PRONOUNS, *WHERE*, AND *WHEN*

Combine the pairs of sentences, using **who(m)**, **which**, **that**, **whose**, **where**, *or* **when**. *Make the second sentence in each pair an adjective clause. Make any other necessary changes.*

1. Jean M. Auel wrote a novel. I enjoyed reading it.

   Jean M. Auel wrote a novel which I enjoyed reading.

2. *The Clan of the Cave Bear* tells the story of a clan of prehistoric people. Auel started researching the book in 1977.

   _____

3. It took a lot of work to learn about these prehistoric people. Auel wanted to understand the prehistoric people's lives.

   _____

4. The clan lived during the Ice Age. Glaciers covered large parts of the earth then.

   _____

5. The people lived near the shores of the Black Sea. There are a lot of large caves there.

   _____

6. The clan made their home in a large cave. Bears had lived in the cave.

   _____

(continued)

7. The task of hunting had great importance in the life of the Cave Bear Clan. The men were responsible for the task of hunting.

   _____

8. One aspect of their lives was their technical skill. Auel describes that aspect well.

   _____

9. She learned some of the arts. Prehistoric people had practiced them.

   _____

10. In her preface, Auel thanks a man. She studied the art of making stone tools with him.

    _____

11. She also thanks an Arctic survival expert. She met him while she was doing research.

    _____

12. He taught her to make a snow cave on Mt. Hood. She spent one January night there.

    _____

13. She went through a difficult time. She couldn't write then.

    _____

14. A fiction writer inspired her to finish her book. She attended the writer's lecture.

    _____

15. Jean Auel's novel remains popular with fans around the world. She published the novel in 1980.

    _____

4 | OPTIONAL DELETIONS OF RELATIVE PRONOUNS

In five of the sentences in Exercise 3, the relative pronoun can be deleted. Rewrite the sentences below with the relative pronoun deleted.

1. *Jean M. Auel wrote a novel I enjoyed reading.*

2. _____

3. _____

4. _____

5. _____

5 | EDITING

Read this student's book report. There are nine mistakes in the use of adjective clauses. The first mistake is already corrected. Find and correct eight more.

Jorge Ramos

English 220

    For my book report, I read *The Clan of the Cave Bear*, ~~that~~ which Jean M. Auel wrote after several years of research. In this novel about the life of prehistoric people, the main character is Ayla. She is found by a wandering clan after an earthquake kills her family. The same earthquake destroyed the cave in which this clan had lived, and they are searching for another home. The clan leader wants to leave Ayla to die. She is an Other—a human which language and culture his clan doesn't understand. However, the leader's sister Iza, Ayla soon calls Mother, adopts her.

    The story takes place at a time where human beings are still evolving. Ayla is a new kind of human. Her brain, which she can use it to predict and make plans, is different from Iza's and other clan members'. Their brains are adapted to memory, not new learning, whom they fear and distrust. At first, Ayla brings luck to the clan. She accidentally wanders into a place where they find a large cave, perfect for their new home. She is educated by Iza, who's great knowledge everyone respects. The skills that Iza passes on to Ayla include healing and magic, as well as finding food, cooking, and sewing. However, Ayla's powers make it impossible for her to stay with the clan. She learns to hunt, a skill where women are forbidden to practice. Her uncle, that she loves very much, allows her to stay with the clan, but after he dies, she loses his protection. Another earthquake, for which she is blamed, destroys the clan's home, and she is forced to leave.

Workbook Answer Key

In this answer key, where the contracted form is given, the full form is often also correct, and where the full form is given, the contracted form is often also correct.

UNIT 1 (pages 1–4)

1

2. ask, asking
3. buys, buying
4. come, comes
5. do, doing
6. eats, eating
7. employ, employs
8. fly, flies
9. forgets, forgetting
10. have, having
11. hurries, hurrying
12. lie, lies
13. opens, opening
14. rains, raining
15. reaches, reaching
16. say, saying
17. ties, tying
18. travel, travels

2

A. 2. Are . . . taking
3. is studying
4. 's
5. remember
6. look

B. 1. Do . . . know
2. teaches
3. 's working
4. does . . . mean
5. don't believe

C. 1. do . . . spell
2. have
3. looks

D. 1. are . . . sitting
2. don't seem
3. 'm trying
4. doesn't like
5. writes
6. is
7. 's beginning

E. 1. Do . . . want
2. is studying
3. does . . . do
4. analyzes
5. write
6. sign

3

2. doesn't know
3. is focusing
4. is writing
5. looks
6. studies
7. believe
8. gives
9. are using OR use
10. does . . . hope OR is . . . hoping
11. look
12. tells
13. Does . . . lean
14. indicates
15. represents
16. is planning
17. doesn't leave
18. avoids
19. show
20. 's
21. is investigating
22. thinks
23. takes
24. warns
25. doesn't guarantee

4

Hi!

Well, I'm here at my new school, and ~~I'm~~ *I* ~~liking~~ *like* it very much. I'm ~~study~~ *studying* English this semester, but the classes are really different from our English classes in Korea. My teachers ~~doesn't~~ *don't* know how to speak Korean, and my classmates ~~are coming~~ *come* from countries all around the world, so we use English all the time. That ~~is meaning~~ *means* that I'm getting a lot of good practice these days.

Although I'm very happy, ~~I'm~~ *I* sometimes ~~having~~ *have* problems. ~~I'm not~~ *I don't* understand my classmates' names because they don't look or sound like Korean names. I always ask the same questions: "What's your name?" and "How ~~you~~ *do you* spell it?" My teachers want me to call them by their first names. It's difficult for me to treat my teachers so informally, but I *'m* trying. Slowly but surely, I'm getting accustomed to my life here.

I miss you a lot. ~~Your~~ *You're* still my favorite English teacher.
Hye Lee

UNIT 2 (pages 5–8)

1

2. apply
3. was, were
4. became
5. carried
6. developed
7. eat
8. fell
9. feel
10. got
11. grew
12. lived
13. meet
14. pay
15. permitted
16. planned
17. send
18. slept

AK-1

2

2. met	26. became
3. asked	27. was dating
4. Was	28. didn't seem
5. did . . . notice	29. heard
6. Were . . . going	30. was whispering
7. found	31. got
8. didn't fall	32. told
9. were working	33. wanted
10. met	34. changed
11. hired	35. realized
12. was trying	36. didn't stop
13. was	37. broke up
14. was feeling OR felt	38. asked
15. was pretending OR pretended	39. was moving
16. thought	40. saw
17. wanted	41. was sitting
18. was working	42. was trying
19. came	43. jumped
20. didn't ask	44. thought
21. solved	45. didn't ask
22. stopped	46. was helping
23. fell	47. seemed
24. were taking	48. saw
25. met	49. introduced
	50. invited

3

December 16

I'm really glad that I ~~was deciding~~ *decided* to rent this apartment. I almost ~~wasn't~~ *didn't* move here because the rent is a little high, but I'm happy to be here. All the other apartments I looked at ~~were seeming~~ *seemed* so small, and the neighborhoods just weren't as beautiful as this one. And moving wasn't as bad as I feared. My original plan was to take a week off from work, but when Hakim ~~was offering~~ *offered* to help, I didn't need so much time. What a great brother! We ~~were moving~~ *moved* everything into the apartment in two days. The man next door was really nice to us. On the second day, he even helped Hakim with some of the heavy furniture. His name is Jared. I ~~don't~~ *didn't* even unpack the kitchen stuff last weekend because I was so tired. Last night I ~~walking~~ *walked* Mitzi for only two blocks. When I came back, Jared ~~stood~~ *was standing* downstairs. I think I made him nervous because he ~~was dropping~~ *dropped* his mail when he saw me. I'd like to ask him over for coffee this weekend (in order to thank him), but everything is still in boxes. Maybe in a couple of weeks . . .

UNIT 3 (pages 9–14)

1

2. brought, brought
3. chose, chosen
4. delayed, delayed
5. felt, felt
6. found, found
7. finished, finished
8. got, gotten
9. graduated, graduated
10. hid, hidden
11. noticed, noticed
12. omitted, omitted
13. owned, owned
14. read, read
15. replied, replied
16. ripped, ripped
17. showed, shown
18. spoke, spoken

2

2. She graduated from college in 1999.
3. She's been reporting OR She's reported crime news since 2002.
4. Recently, she's been researching crime in schools.
5. She's been working on her master's degree since 2002.
6. Her father worked for the Broadfield Police Department for 20 years.
7. Simon Pohlig moved to Broadfield in 1997.
8. He's owned Sharney's Restaurant since 1999.
9. He coached basketball for the Boys and Girls Club for two years.
10. He's written two cookbooks for children.
11. He's been planning a local television show for several months.
12. The groom's mother has been serving OR has served as president of TLC Meals, Inc. for two years.

3

2. applied
3. has been working OR has worked
4. has written
5. found, was
6. has attended
7. began, received
8. went on
9. has taken
10. started
11. didn't get
12. decided
13. hasn't received
14. lived
15. has lived OR has been living
16. has recommended OR recommended

17. left
18. hasn't told
19. didn't slant
20. explained

4

My son and his girlfriend have ~~made~~ *been making* wedding plans for the past few months. At first I was delighted, but last week I ~~have heard~~ *heard* something that changed my feelings. It seems that our future daughter-in-law has ~~been deciding~~ *decided* to keep her own last name after the wedding. Her reasons: First, she doesn't want to "lose her identity." Her parents ~~have named~~ *named* her 31 years ago, and she ~~was~~ *has been* Donna Esposito since then. She sees no reason to change now. Second, she is a member of the Rockland Symphony Orchestra and she ~~performed~~ *has performed* OR *has been performing* with them for eight years. As a result, she ~~already became~~ *has already become* known professionally by her maiden name.

John, when I~~'ve gotten~~ *got* married, I didn't think of keeping my maiden name. I ~~have felt~~ *felt* so proud when I became "Mrs. Smith." We named our son after my father, but our surname showed that we three were a family.

I've ~~been reading~~ *read* two articles about this trend, and I can now understand her decision to use her maiden name professionally. But I still can't understand why she wants to use it socially.

My husband and I ~~tried~~ *have tried* many times to hide our hurt feelings, but it's been getting harder. I want to tell her and my son what I think, but my husband says it's none of our business.

My son ~~didn't say~~ *hasn't said* anything so far, so we don't know how he feels. ~~Have we been making~~ *Have we made* the right choice by keeping quiet?

A Concerned Mother Who ~~Hasn't Been Saying~~ *Hasn't Said* One Word Yet

UNIT 4 (pages 15–23)

1

2. break, broken
3. cutting, cut
4. doing, done
5. entertaining, entertained
6. fight, fighting
7. forgiving, forgiven
8. leading, led
9. planning, planned
10. practicing, practiced
11. quitting, quit
12. seek, seeking
13. sink, sinking
14. stealing, stolen
15. sweeping, swept
16. swimming, swum
17. telling, told
18. withdraw, withdrawing

2

2. had . . . won
3. hadn't learned
4. hadn't brought
5. had found
6. had . . . established
7. had earned
8. had offered
9. had . . . written
10. had received
11. hadn't gotten
12. had met
13. had starred
14. had opened
15. had become
16. had finished

3

2. Had he flown; No, he hadn't.
3. Had he arrived; No, he hadn't.
4. Had he received; Yes, he had.
5. Had he met; Yes, he had.
6. Had he eaten; No, he hadn't.
7. Had he prepared; Yes, he had.

4

2. hadn't been doing
3. had been raining
4. had been eating
5. hadn't been drinking
6. had been crying
7. had been laughing
8. had been washing OR had been doing
9. had been listening
10. hadn't been paying

5

2. How long had he been living in Hollywood when he finally found an acting job?
3. Had he really been working as a cook in a fast-food restaurant when he became a successful actor?
4. Where had he been studying when he decided to enroll in classes at the Actors Studio Drama School?
5. Why had he been taking courses in accounting when he began his acting classes?

6. How long had he been thinking about working behind the cameras when he directed his first film?
7. Had he been looking for investors for a long time when he started his own production company?

6

2. had decided
3. had been swimming
4. had . . . lost
5. had had
6. had been searching
7. hadn't found
8. had been working
9. had been living
10. had appeared
11. had been making

7

2. Before she became a professional dancer, she had been studying at a business college.
3. She had been a dancer on the popular TV show *In Living Color* before she danced with Janet Jackson.
4. By the time she appeared in her first major film, she had been dancing professionally for several years.
5. When she starred in *Selena*, she had already finished the action film *Money Train*.
6. She had divorced her first husband by the time she started her singing career.
7. She had made several films before she got the name "J. Lo."
8. When she set a record for #1 movie and #1 album on the same weekend, she had been dating Sean "P. Diddy" Combs.
9. When she filmed *Maid in Manhattan*, she hadn't ended her relationship with her second husband yet.
10. By the time she fell in love with Ben Affleck, she had gotten married twice.
11. Their movie *Gigli* had failed at the box office by the time she called off her wedding to Ben Affleck.
12. She married actor and singer Marc Anthony after she had called off her wedding to Ben Affleck.

UNIT 5 (pages 24–28)

1

2. I'll come
3. Are you taking
4. I'll hand
5. It's going to fall
6. You're moving
7. Are you driving, We're flying
8. are you getting, We're going to take
9. I'll drive, we're going to have

2

2. will be living
3. are going to be parking
4. aren't going to be preparing
5. will be eating
6. won't be driving
7. will be walking
8. will be moving
9. will . . . be saving
10. aren't going to be buying
11. aren't going to be paying
12. won't be worrying
13. will be providing
14. are going to be attending
15. will be helping
16. (will be) providing
17. are going to be seeing

3

2. are you going to be using the lawn mower tomorrow? No, I'm not.
3. will we be getting new washers?
4. will you be going to the post office tomorrow? Yes, I will.
5. are you going to be making?
6. Will the entertainment committee be planning anything else in the near future? Yes, we will.
7. Are we going to be meeting then? No, we aren't.

4

2. will be meeting with . . . faxes reports
3. attends . . . will be having a phone conference with John Smith
4. has (OR eats) . . . will be having (OR eating) lunch with Jack Allen
5. will be billing clients . . . drafts
6. picks up . . . will be taking Saril to the dentist
7. will be shopping for . . . takes Dursan to the barber
8. pays . . . will be cutting the grass

5

I ~~go~~ *'m going* to Jack's with the kids in a few minutes. We'll be ~~play~~ *playing* cards until 10:30 or so. While ~~we'll~~ *we* play cards, Jack's daughter will be watching the kids. It ~~will~~ *'s going to* rain, so I closed all the windows. Don't forget to watch "CSI"! It ~~'ll start~~ *starts* OR *'s starting* at 10:00. I *'ll* call you after the card game because by the time we get home, you ~~'re sleeping~~ *'ll be sleeping*. Enjoy your evening.

UNIT 6 (pages 29–33)

1

2. will have completed
3. will have helped
4. 'll have been using OR 'll have used
5. 'll have bought
6. 'll have wrapped
7. won't have planned
8. won't have decided
9. 'll . . . have been arguing OR 'll . . . have argued
10. won't have wasted
11. 'll have completed
12. 'll have had
13. 'll have participated
14. (will have) redecorated
15. 'll have made
16. 'll have done
17. 'll have straightened
18. 'll have packed
19. 'll have been explaining

2

1. Yes, I will (have).
2. will you have been performing
3. will you have sewn
4. will the kids have been waiting OR will the kids have waited
5. will the paint have dried; No, it won't (have).
6. Will the cleaners have delivered; Yes, they will (have).
7. will we have been living OR will we have lived

3

2. A: How long will Aida have been walking by August 31?
   B: She'll have been walking (for) a month.
3. A: How many rooms will Arnie have painted by August 5?
   B: He'll have painted three rooms.
4. A: How long will Arnie have been painting downstairs by August 15?
   B: He'll have been painting downstairs (for) four days.
5. A: On August 16, will Arnie have left for his dentist appointment by 4:00?
   B: Yes, he will (have).
6. A: Will Aida have unpacked all the fall clothing by August 23?
   B: No, she won't (have).
7. A: How long will Aida have been driving in the carpool by August 19?
   B: She'll have been driving in the carpool (for) two weeks.
8. A: How many quarts of blueberries will Corrie have picked by August 19?
   B: She'll have picked three quarts of blueberries.
9. A: How many pies will Aida have baked by August 21?
   B: She'll have baked six pies.
10. A: Will they have finished packing for the trip by August 31?
    B: Yes, they will (have).

UNIT 7 (pages 34–38)

1

2. doesn't it?; No, it doesn't.
3. is it?; No, it isn't.
4. haven't you?; Yes, I have.
5. does it?; Yes, it does.
6. didn't you?; Yes, I did.
7. doesn't it?; Yes, it does.
8. can I?; Yes, you can.
9. will you?; No, I won't.
10. don't you?; Yes, I do.

2

2. Didn't Greenwood build a public beach? No, it didn't.
3. Isn't there an airport in Greenwood? No, there isn't.
4. Can't you see live theater performances in Greenwood? No, you can't.
5. Don't people in Greenwood shop at a nearby mall? Yes, they do.
6. Isn't the average rent in Greenwood under $700? Yes, it is.
7. Hasn't Greenwood been a town for more than a hundred years? Yes, it has.
8. Aren't they going to build a baseball stadium in Greenwood? Yes, they are.

3

A. 3. isn't it
B. 1. have you
   2. Didn't . . . fill out
   3. shouldn't we
C. 1. Isn't
   2. Didn't . . . use to be
   3. had it
D. 1. aren't they
   2. have you
   3. Can't . . . take

4

3. This is a good building, isn't it? OR Isn't this a good building?
4. The owner takes good care of it, doesn't he? OR Doesn't the owner take good care of it?
5. He's just finished renovations on the lobby, hasn't he? OR Hasn't he just finished renovations on the lobby?
6. He didn't paint our apartment before we moved in, did he?
7. He doesn't talk very much, does he?
8. The rent won't increase next year, will it?
9. Some new people will be moving into Apartment 1B, won't they? OR Won't some new people be moving into Apartment 1B?
10. This is a really nice place to live, isn't it? OR Isn't this a really nice place to live?

UNIT 8 (pages 39–42)

1

3. so
4. too
5. neither
6. had
7. but
8. aren't
9. didn't
10. and
11. too

2

A. 2. didn't either
   3. am too
   4. did too
   5. so did
   6. but . . . don't
B. 1. but . . . didn't
   2. neither had
   3. so did
   4. but . . . wasn't
C. 1. are too
   2. so will

3

2. but Pleucadeuc wasn't
3. and neither does Beijing OR and Beijing doesn't either
4. but the Pleucadeuc and Beijing festivals are
5. and Pleucadeuc will too OR and so will Pleucadeuc
6. and so should participants at Pleucadeuc OR and participants at Pleucadeuc should too
7. and the Beijing festival doesn't either OR and neither does the Beijing festival
8. and so does Pleucadeuc OR and Pleucadeuc does too
9. but triplets, quads, and quints don't
10. and neither did Beijing OR and Beijing didn't either
11. and their families have too OR and so have their families

UNIT 9 (pages 43–49)

1

3. to watch
4. to watch
5. to watch
6. to watch OR watching
7. to watch
8. watching
9. to watch
10. watching
11. to watch OR watching
12. watching
13. watching
14. watching
15. to watch
16. watching
17. watching
18. watching
19. to watch
20. to watch

2

2. watching
3. to recall
4. hearing
5. to calm
6. Sponsoring
7. to limit
8. to participate
9. creating
10. to preview
11. having
12. to believe
13. viewing
14. interacting
15. to behave
16. to produce
17. limiting OR to limit
18. not permitting
19. to watch
20. to understand
21. making
22. to develop
23. (to) get rid of
24. to offer
25. to advertise
26. to decrease
27. not to continue
28. to avoid OR avoiding
29. not to pay
30. to investigate
31. to schedule
32. turning on

3

2. unwilling to change
3. used to putting
4. fed up with seeing
5. likely to hit
6. force . . . to rate
7. hesitate to tell
8. decided to run
9. stopped showing
10. dislike turning off
11. insist on changing
12. forbid . . . to turn on
13. permit . . . to tune in
14. consider owning
15. advise . . . to do
16. keep communicating
17. hesitate to ask
18. agreeing to speak

4

2. A V-chip interferes with Annie's (OR Annie) watching violent shows.
3. *Reading Rainbow* encourages them to get interested in books.
4. Her father told Jennifer not to watch cop shows anymore.
5. The teacher recommended their watching *Nick News*.
6. Bob didn't (OR doesn't) remember their (OR them) seeing that game.
7. Sharif's parents persuaded him not to watch *Z-Men*.
8. The mother insisted on Sara's (OR Sara) turning off the TV.
9. Aziza wanted (OR wants) Ben to change the channel.
10. Nick can't get used to Paul's (OR Paul) watching a Spanish-language news program.

5

I'm tired of ~~hear~~ *hearing* that violence on TV causes violence at home, in school, and on the streets. Almost all young people watch TV, but not all of them are involved in committing crimes! In fact, very few people choose ~~acting~~ *to act* in violent ways. ~~To watch~~ *Watching* TV, therefore, is not the cause.

Groups like the American Medical Society should stop making a point of ~~to tell~~ *telling* people what to watch. If we want ~~living~~ *to live* in a free society, it is necessary ~~having~~ *to have* freedom of choice. Children need to ~~learn~~ *to learn* values from their parents. It should be the parents' responsibility ~~deciding~~ *to decide* what their child can or cannot watch. The government and other interest groups should avoid ~~to interfere~~ *interfering* in these personal decisions. Limiting our freedom of choice is not the answer. If parents teach their children ~~respecting~~ *to respect* life, children can enjoy ~~to watch~~ *watching* TV without any negative effects.

UNIT 10 (pages 50–54)

1

2. let	5. make	8. help
3. help	6. get	9. gets
4. makes	7. have	10. let

11. makes	13. have
12. help	14. make

2

2. you keep
3. you (to) decide
4. them give
5. her to do
6. them take care of
7. them to realize
8. him to calm down
9. her play
10. him (to) adjust
11. him spend
12. him to obey
13. him understand
14. you (to) relax
15. us provide

3

2. got him to agree to adopt a dog or a cat.
3. let him make the choice.
4. made him do some research on pet care.
5. didn't help him do the research. OR didn't help him to do the research.
6. got her to fill out and sign the adoption application forms.
7. had him explain the adoption process (to her).
8. didn't make him pay the adoption fees.

4

Thanks for staying in touch. Your e-mails always make me ~~to smile~~ *smile*—even when I'm feeling stressed. Knowing that I have a good friend like you really helps me relax and not take things so seriously. My classes are difficult this semester. I still can't believe that three of my professors are making ~~them~~ *me* OR *us* write 20-page papers.

At the end of last semester, my roommates and I decided to get a dog. Actually, my roommates made the decision and then got me ~~go~~ *to go* along with it. I made them promise to take care of the dog, but guess who's doing most of the work! Don't misunderstand me. I love Ellie and appreciate what a great companion she is. I take her for a walk every morning and every night and ~~make~~ *let* her run and play in the park near our apartment as often as I can because I know how much she enjoys it. Still, I wish I could have my roommates ~~to spend~~ *spend* just an hour a week with "our" dog. At this point, I can't even get them

to feed
~~feeding~~ Ellie, and now they want to move to an
apartment complex that won't let us ~~to have~~ *have* a dog.
I think I'm going to have to choose whether to live
with my roommates or with Ellie—and I think I'm
going to choose Ellie!
Take care. I'll write again soon.

UNIT 11 (pages 55–58)

1

2. up
3. over
4. ahead
5. out
6. down
7. over
8. out
9. back
10. out
11. up
12. down
13. up
14. down
15. off
16. up

2

2. cut down
3. put together
4. burns up
5. sets up
6. puts on
7. gets together
8. give out
9. go out
10. go back
11. throws away

3

A. 2. pick them out
B. 1. empty out the money and everything else in your pockets
   2. throw it away
C. 1. set the firecrackers off
   2. keeps them away
D. 1. hanging these streamers up
   2. set it up
E. 1. write down all of the resolutions that I make each year
   2. gave them up

4

Wake ~~out~~ *up* earlier. (No later than 7:30!)
Work out at the gym at least 3 times a week.
Lose 5 pounds. (Give ~~over~~ *up* eating so many desserts.)

Be more conscious of the environment:
—Don't throw ~~down~~ *away* OR *out* newspapers. Recycle them.
—Save energy. Turn ~~on~~ *off* OR *out* the lights when I leave the apartment.

Straighten up my room:
—Hang ~~out~~ *up* my clothes when I take ~~off them~~ *them off*.
—Put my books back where they belong.
—Give some of my old books and clothing that I no longer wear ~~away~~ *away*.

Don't put off doing my homework assignments.
Hand ~~in them~~ *them in* on time!

Read more.

Use the dictionary more. (Look ~~over~~ *up* words I don't know.)

When someone calls and leaves a message, call them back right away. Don't put ~~off it~~ *it off*!

Get to know my neighbors. Ask them for coffee ~~over~~ *over*.

UNIT 12 (pages 59–63)

1

2. over
3. out
4. off
5. in (on) OR by
6. out
7. on
8. into
9. up
10. down
11. into
12. back
13. out
14. on
15. out
16. down

2

A. 2. figured out
   3. catch on
   4. turning on
   5. teamed up with
   6. help . . . out
   7. go off
   8. takes away
   9. turn . . . off
B. 1. keep up with
   2. end up
   3. put . . . away
   4. use up
   5. found out
   6. pick out
   7. look over
   8. watch out for

3

2. get along (well) with him
3. run into her
4. straighten it up
5. gotten together with them
6. pick them out OR pick some out
7. count on them
8. bring it out
9. picked it up
10. turn it down

11. cover them up
12. stuck to it
13. put them away
14. turn it on
15. figure it out

4

Crossword:
Across: 4. LEAVES, 7. DESIRE, 11. CONFUSE, 13. CALCULATE, 16. RISE, 17. OMIT, 18. INVENT, 19. PENS, 23. TELEPHONE, 25. STAY, 26. ST, 27. CENTER, 31. CANCEL, 32. AN, 33. PRO, 34. MD, 38. DOES, 40. HAPPEN, 41. ERECT

Down: 1. M, 2. H, 3. W, 5. A, 6. SUBMISSION (?), ... (crossword grid)

UNIT 13 (pages 64–67)

1

2. whose
3. who
4. who
5. that
6. that
7. whose
8. that
9. who
10. that
11. whose
12. who
13. that
14. who

2

3. that OR which
4. occur
5. who OR that
6. stay
7. who OR that
8. make
9. that OR which
10. don't change
11. that OR which
12. remain
13. whose
14. come
15. who OR that
16. are
17. that OR which
18. helps
19. that OR which
20. makes
21. that OR which
22. holds
23. that OR which
24. surrounds
25. who OR that
26. know
27. that OR which
28. has
29. who OR that
30. has
31. whose
32. are
33. who OR that
34. consider
35. who OR that
36. seize

3

2. She was visiting her favorite aunt, whose apartment was right across from mine.
3. I was immediately attracted to Rebecca because of her smile, which was full of warmth and good humor.
4. I could see that Rebecca was a terrific woman whose interests were similar to mine. OR I could see that Rebecca was a terrific woman, whose interests were similar to mine.
5. Ballroom dancing, which was very popular in those days, was one of our favorite activities.
6. We also enjoyed playing cards with some of our close friends who (OR that) lived in the neighborhood.
7. Our friend Mike, who was a professional skier, taught us how to ski.
8. We got married in a ski lodge that (OR which) was in Vermont.
9. Our marriage, which means a lot to us both, has grown through the years.
10. The love and companionship that (OR which) make us very happy have gotten stronger.
11. Even the bad things that (OR which) have happened have brought us closer together.
12. I really love Rebecca, who is not only my wife but also my best friend.

UNIT 14 (pages 68–73)

1

A. 2. who
B. 1. who
   2. who
   3. whom
C. 1. who
   2. who
   3. whose
D. 1. who
   2. where
   3. whom
E. 1. which
   2. whose
   3. whom
   4. whose
   5. that
F. 1. that
   2. where
   3. who
G. 1. whose
   2. whose
   3. who
   4. which
   5. who
   6. whom

2

2. where
3. thanks
4. whose
5. finds, has found, OR found
6. which OR that
7. writes
8. which OR that
9. reads
10. which OR that
11. face
12. when OR that

13. runs out of OR has run out of
14. when
15. supported
16. which
17. praised
18. which
19. inserted
20. whom
21. feels
22. whom
23. dedicates OR has dedicated
24. where
25. has
26. which OR that
27. are supposed

3

2. *The Clan of the Cave Bear*, which Auel started researching in 1977, tells the story of a clan of prehistoric people.
3. It took a lot of work to learn about these prehistoric people, whose lives Auel wanted to understand.
4. The clan lived during the Ice Age, when glaciers covered large parts of the earth.
5. The people lived near the shores of the Black Sea, where there are a lot of large caves.
6. The clan made their home in a large cave where bears had lived.
7. The task of hunting, which the men were responsible for, had great importance in the life of the Cave Bear Clan. OR The task of hunting, for which the men were responsible, had great importance in the life of the Cave Bear Clan.
8. One aspect of their lives which (OR that) Auel describes well was their technical skill.
9. She learned some of the arts that (OR which) prehistoric people had practiced.
10. In her preface, Auel thanks a man with whom she studied the art of making stone tools. OR Auel thanks a man who (OR whom) (OR that) she studied the art of making stone tools with.
11. She also thanks an Arctic survival expert who (OR whom) (OR that) she met while she was doing research.
12. He taught her to make a snow cave on Mt. Hood, where she spent one January night.
13. She went through a difficult time when she couldn't write.
14. A fiction writer whose lecture she attended inspired her to finish her book.
15. Jean Auel's novel, which she published in 1980, remains popular with fans around the world.

4

Sentence 8: One aspect of their lives Auel describes well was their technical skill.
Sentence 9: She learned some of the arts prehistoric people had practiced.
Sentence 10: In her preface, Auel thanks a man she studied the art of making stone tools with.
Sentence 11: She also thanks an Arctic survival expert she met while she was doing research.

5

For my book report, I read *The Clan of the Cave Bear,* ~~that~~ *which* Jean M. Auel wrote after several years of research. In this novel about the life of prehistoric people, the main character is Ayla. She is found by a wandering clan after an earthquake kills her family. The same earthquake destroyed the cave in which this clan had lived, and they are searching for another home. The clan leader wants to leave Ayla to die. She is an Other—a human ~~which~~ *whose* language and culture his clan doesn't understand. However, the leader's sister Iza, *who* OR *whom* Ayla soon calls Mother, adopts her.

The story takes place at a time ~~where~~ *when* human beings are still evolving. Ayla is a new kind of human. Her brain, which she can use ✗ to predict and make plans, is different from Iza's and other clan members'. Their brains are adapted to memory, not new learning, ~~whom~~ *which* they fear and distrust. At first, Ayla brings luck to the clan. She accidentally wanders into a place where they find a large cave, perfect for their new home. She is educated by Iza, ~~who's~~ *whose* great knowledge everyone respects. The skills that Iza passes on to Ayla include healing and magic, as well as finding food, cooking, and sewing. However, Ayla's powers make it impossible for her to stay with the clan. She learns to hunt, a skill ~~where~~ *which* OR *that* OR (pronoun deleted) women are forbidden to practice. Her uncle, ~~that~~ *who* OR *whom* she loves very much, allows her to stay with the clan, but after he dies, she loses his protection. Another earthquake, for which she is blamed, destroys the clan's home, and she is forced to leave.

UNIT 15 (pages 74–77)

1

2. necessity
3. future possibility
4. assumption
5. assumption
6. necessity
7. prohibition
8. advice
9. future possibility
10. ability
11. prohibition

12. advice
13. future possibility
14. ability
15. advice

2

2. may not be
3. were able to fulfill
4. could catch
5. 'd better not jump
6. might see
7. can watch
8. may not sound
9. could harm
10. might shoot
11. doesn't have to use
12. 's able to catch
13. should take care of
14. might not mind

3

2. Should, 'd better not
3. 've got to, can
4. may not
5. must not, ought to
6. has to, should, may
7. 'd better not, weren't able to
8. could, must
9. 'd better, might not
10. can, were we able to
11. 've got to, don't have to
12. can't, should, have got to

4

I have watched all of your shows several times, and I must ~~to be~~ *be* one of your biggest fans. The first time I saw you stick your hand in a nest of poisonous snakes, I ~~might not~~ *couldn't* believe my eyes. In fact, some people have come to the conclusion that you ~~ought to~~ *must* OR *have (got) to* be crazy to take risks like that. But they still ~~don't able to~~ *aren't able to* OR *can't* stop watching! Since your show started, you ~~can~~ *have been able to* make a lot of people interested in nature. I am one of those people.

I am a high school senior, and because of your shows, I might major in zoology in college. I'm going to take general courses the first two years, so I ~~must not~~ *don't have to* choose my major yet. One of my concerns is that there ~~couldn't~~ *might not* OR *may not* be any jobs in zoology when I graduate. What is your opinion? Will there be a lot of jobs in this field in the next few years? My other problem is that my parents don't want me to work with animals. They haven't actually said, "You ~~don't have to~~ *must not* OR *can't* major in zoology," but they are very worried. What can I ~~to tell~~ *tell* them? I hope you will be able to find the time to answer this letter.

UNIT 16 (pages 78–81)

1

2. could . . . have done
3. Should . . . have let
4. Yes, you should have.
5. could have given
6. might have discussed
7. should . . . have handled
8. shouldn't have adjusted
9. ought to have faced
10. should have tried
11. Should . . . have ignored
12. No, you shouldn't have.
13. ought to have told
14. might have acted
15. Should . . . have complained
16. No, you shouldn't have.
17. ought to have been able to
18. shouldn't have spent
19. shouldn't have called
20. might have focused
21. could have admitted

2

2. They ought to have created a budget with some "personal money" for each partner.
3. He might have treated her attitude with respect.
4. She shouldn't have accused him of irresponsibility.
5. They should have planned ahead.
6. They could have scheduled time alone with each other.
7. He shouldn't have sulked.
8. They might have started with small tasks.
9. They could have provided containers to help organize the toys.
10. He shouldn't have given up and done it himself.

3

I think my new roommate and I have both realized our mistakes. Reggie ~~should~~ *shouldn't* have demanded the biggest room in the apartment as soon as he arrived. He ought *to* have spoken to me first—after all, I've lived here longer than he has. On the other hand, I really shouldn't ~~shout~~ *have shouted* at him as soon as he asked me. I could have ~~control~~ *controlled* my temper and just talked to him about the problem first. I felt really bad about that—until he invited friends over the night before I had to take a test!

AK-11

Then I got so angry, I couldn't sleep. He might have ~~asks~~ *asked* me first! I ~~oughta~~ *ought to* have said something right away, but I didn't want to yell again. Of course, some of my habits make Reggie mad too. For example, I could've started washing my dishes when he moved in, but I just let them pile up in the sink. That was pretty gross—I definitely shouldn't have ~~did~~ *done* that. But ~~should have he~~ *should he have* dumped all the dirty dishes in my bedroom? He might ^*have* found a better way to tell me he was annoyed. Last week, he wanted to talk about our problems. As soon as we started, I realized we should have talked much sooner. Things have worked out a lot better since our discussion.

UNIT 17 (pages 82–86)

1

2. couldn't have
3. must have
4. may have
5. must have
6. must have
7. could have
8. may have
9. could have
10. couldn't have
11. had to have

2

2. must not have been
3. had to have felt
4. must have occupied
5. may have traded
6. couldn't have lived
7. may not have lived
8. must have fought
9. may have been
10. might not have produced
11. could have gone
12. might not have had
13. may have suffered
14. could have led
15. might have destroyed
16. could have been

3

2. It must have been
3. He might have
4. He may have
5. She could have
6. It must have been
7. They must have
8. He might not have been
9. It couldn't have been

UNIT 18 (pages 87–91)

1

3. Several employees were fired as a result of the mistake.
4. An article about China was published last month.
5. Al Baker wrote the article.
6. They frequently hire new editors at the newspaper.
7. Marla Jacobson was interviewed by two of the new editors.
8. They gave Marla an assignment on the Philippines.
9. The article was researched thoroughly by Marla.
10. The information fascinated our readers.

2

2. were called
3. is known
4. is made up
5. are considered
6. were formed
7. were not given
8. is (OR was) called
9. is (OR was) named

3

3. are inhabited
4. are found
5. damage
6. cause
7. was covered
8. cover
9. contain
10. are found
11. are used
12. inhabit

4

3. were followed by groups from Indonesia
4. are spoken
5. are understood by speakers of other dialects
6. was declared by President Manuel Quezon
7. is spoken by more than 70 million people
8. is taught
9. are spoken (by people)
10. is used

5

3. Where are fruits and nuts grown? They're grown in the north (OR northeast) and in the central part of the country.
4. Where is logging done? It's done in the east.
5. What animals are raised? Sheep, cattle, and llamas are raised.
6. Are llamas found in the east? No, they aren't.
7. Are potatoes grown? Yes, they are.
8. Where is rubber produced? It's produced in the north.

9. Where is oil found? It's found in the south, east, and west (OR northwest).
10. Is wheat grown in the north? No, it isn't.
11. Are cattle raised in the east? Yes, they are.

UNIT 19 (pages 92–95)

1

2. Some new airports may be constructed on islands.
3. They might put passenger facilities on decks under the runways.
4. A lot of space could be saved that way.
5. The Japanese had to build an island airport in Osaka Bay.
6. At the old airport, all the air traffic couldn't be handled.
7. Huge amounts of earth had to be moved from nearby mountains.
8. International visitors will be impressed by Hong Kong's island airport.
9. Travelers can reach the airport easily.
10. Before, Lantau could be reached only by ferry.

2

2. can be connected
3. will be started
4. may be completed
5. are going to be linked
6. can . . . be carried
7. may not be driven
8. are able to be transported
9. could be joined
10. will be called
11. will . . . be built
12. must be bridged
13. have to be developed
14. will be built
15. will be included
16. might not be fulfilled
17. can't be avoided
18. will be solved

3

2. No, they can't
3. Do . . . have to be occupied
4. No, they don't
5. Should . . . be purchased
6. Yes, they should
7. Is . . . going to be expanded
8. Yes, it is
9. Will . . . be offered
10. Yes, they will
11. Can . . . be purchased
12. Yes, it can

UNIT 20 (pages 96–101)

1

2. I'm having (OR getting) my computer repaired.
3. I had (OR got) my car checked by my favorite mechanic at Majestic Motors.
4. We've just had (OR gotten) our windows cleaned.
5. We're going to have (OR get) our grass cut.
6. We must have (OR get) our house painted.
7. We should have (OR get) our electrical wiring checked.
8. We will probably have (OR get) most of the work on our house done by Northtown Contractors.
9. We might have (OR get) a new porch built (by them) too.
10. The neighbors had better have (OR get) their (OR the) roof fixed.

2

2. have . . . completed
3. have . . . done
4. get . . . tested
5. have . . . replaced
6. have . . . investigated
7. had . . . installed
8. get . . . replaced
9. didn't have . . . done
10. had . . . tested
11. have . . . checked out
12. have . . . stopped
13. have . . . put
14. getting . . . publicized

3

2. How often do you get it done?
3. Did you get it winterized?
4. Have you ever gotten snow tires put on?
5. Are you going to get (OR Will you get OR Are you getting) snow tires put on for the trip?
6. How many times have you gotten it checked since then?
7. Why do you get the work done there?

4

3. He didn't have (OR get) the undercarriage inspected.
4. He had (OR got) the body and chassis lubricated.

5. He had (OR got) the air filter inspected.
6. He didn't have (OR get) the air filter replaced.
7. He didn't have (OR get) the tires rotated.
8. He didn't have (OR get) the timing and engine speed adjusted.
9. He had (OR got) the automatic transmission serviced.
10. He had (OR got) the cooling system flushed.

5

We've just ~~have~~ *had* our furniture brought over from the apartment, and we're really excited about moving into our "new" (but very old) house. A 19th-century millionaire had this place ~~build~~ *built* for his daughter ~~by a builder~~. We were able to afford it because it's a real "fixer-upper." It needs to ~~has~~ *have* a lot of work done. We've already gotten the roof ~~fix~~ *fixed*, but we're not having the outside ~~painting~~ *painted* until fall. After we get ~~repaired the plumbing~~ *the plumbing repaired*, we'll paint the inside ourselves (we can't paint over those big water stains until the plumbers finish their work). It sounds awful, but just wait until you see it. There's a fireplace in every bedroom—we're ~~get~~ *getting* OR *going to get* the chimneys cleaned before winter. And the windows are huge. In fact, they're so large that we can't wash them ourselves, so yesterday we had ~~done them~~ *them done* professionally.

As you can imagine, we've both been pretty busy, but we'd love to see you. Are you brave enough to visit us?

UNIT 21 (pages 102–106)

1

3. That's right.
4. That's wrong. If you travel in September, your ticket costs more than if you travel in October.
5. That's wrong. If you fly in May, you pay off-season rates.
6. That's wrong. If you buy a one-way ticket, you pay more than half the cost of a round-trip ticket.
7. That's right.
8. That's right.
9. That's wrong. If you leave from Washington, you pay the same fare as from Philadelphia.
10. That's wrong. If you fly from Philadelphia, you pay a lower fare than from Chicago.

2

3. If you don't want to spend a lot of money getting around in Rome, take public transportation.
4. If you don't like to book hotels in advance, go to one of the Rome Provincial Tourist Offices.
5. If you prefer small hotels, stay at *pensiones*.
6. If your husband is very interested in architecture, you must visit the Palazzo Ducale in Venice.
7. If you love opera, you should attend an open-air performance in Verona's Roman Arena.
8. If you're interested in seeing ancient ruins, you might want to consider a side trip to Ostia Antica.
9. If you plan to take a hair dryer and an electric shaver with you, don't forget to take a transformer and an adapter.
10. If you want to have a really good dinner your first night there, you should try Sabatini's.

3

3. You should bring along copies of your prescriptions if you take prescription medication.
4. Notify the flight attendant or train conductor if you feel sick on board a plane or train.
5. Call your own doctor if you are traveling in your own country when you feel sick.
6. Your hotel can recommend a doctor if you need medical attention in a foreign country.
7. If you experience chest pains, weakness in an arm or leg, or shortness of breath, get yourself to an emergency room.
8. If you're not sure how serious your symptoms are, assume they are serious and take appropriate steps.
9. Don't drive to the hospital if you need to go to the emergency room.
10. If you wear glasses, take an extra pair with you.

UNIT 22 (pages 107–111)

1

b. skip
c. unless
d. exercise
e. If
f. change
g. will be
h. take
i. won't catch
j. has
k. are going to have
l. unless
m. If
n. go

2

2. decide
3. will . . . know OR am . . . going to know
4. go
5. 'll . . . have OR 're . . . going to have
6. Will . . . be able to OR Am . . . going to be able to
7. look
8. Yes, you will. OR Yes, you are.
9. have
10. won't be OR aren't going to be OR 're not going to be
11. ends
12. 'll . . . find OR 're . . . going to find
13. see
14. will . . . tell OR is . . . going to tell
15. Yes, it will. OR Yes, it is.
16. set
17. 'll receive OR 're going to receive
18. shows up
19. will . . . be OR is . . . going to be
20. No, it won't. OR No, it isn't.
21. wash
22. 'll get OR 're going to get
23. want
24. won't do OR 're not going to do OR aren't going to do

3

3. You'll have (OR You're going to have) trouble losing weight unless you get regular exercise.
4. You'll receive (OR You're going to receive) some health benefits if you eat carrots.
5. If you stop eating meat, you'll need (OR you're going to need) something to replace it in your diet.
6. If you have a cold, vitamin C will help (OR is going to help) relieve the symptoms.
7. You'll suffer (OR You're going to suffer) possible negative effects if your body gets too much vitamin A.
8. You won't get (OR You aren't going to get OR You're not going to get) sick if you don't drink exactly eight glasses of water a day.
9. You won't have (OR You aren't going to have OR You're not going to have) a problem going out with wet hair unless you're worried about feeling cold or looking less than perfect.

UNIT 23 (pages 112–118)

1

2. could sleep
3. were
4. offered
5. wouldn't eat
6. 'd be
7. had
8. 'd . . . give
9. didn't need
10. 'd offer
11. weren't
12. didn't need
13. 'd share
14. could offer
15. had
16. would taste
17. would taste
18. put
19. had
20. added
21. would be
22. stirred
23. would be
24. knew
25. ate
26. 'd require

2

2. We wish the soldiers wouldn't keep asking for our food.
3. We wish we didn't have to hide our food from them.
4. We wish we didn't need all our grain to feed the cows.
5. We wish all our beds weren't full.
6. We wish there were enough room for the soldiers.
7. We wish the king would come here to eat with us.
8. We wish we had a larger soup pot.
9. We wish we could have stone soup every day.

3

2. If I had potatoes, I'd make potato soup.
3. If my apartment weren't small, I'd invite people over.
4. If steak weren't expensive, we'd eat it.
5. If my daughter weren't sick, I'd go shopping later today.
6. If I didn't have bad eyesight, I could join the army.
7. If the soup had seasoning in it, it wouldn't taste so bland.
8. If I didn't always hide my money, I'd be able to find it now.
9. If I were rich, I'd take vacations.
10. If I had the recipe, I'd make stone soup.

4

2. If I were you, I'd read a fairy tale.
3. If I were you, I'd try cabbage soup.
4. If I were you, I wouldn't add salt.
5. If I were you, I wouldn't ask for a raise.
6. If I were you, I wouldn't take her to see *Rambo VI* (OR to that movie).
7. If I were you, I'd move.
8. If I were you, I'd eat out.

5

2. Who would look for us if we got lost?
3. Where would we go if it started to rain?
4. Would you be afraid if we saw a bear?
5. If you heard a loud growl, would you be scared?
6. What would you do if you were in my place?
7. What would we do if we ran out of food?
8. If we didn't have any more food, would we make stone soup?

6

It's 11:00 P.M. and I'm still awake. I wish I ~~was~~ *were* home. If I ~~would be~~ *were* home, I would be asleep by now! But here I am in the middle of nowhere. My sleeping bag is really uncomfortable. If I were more comfortable, I ~~will~~ *would* be able to sleep. What ~~do~~ *would* my friends think if they could see me now?

I'm cold, tired, and hungry. I wish I ~~have~~ *had* something to eat. But all the food is locked up in the van, and everyone else is sound asleep. If I ~~would have~~ *had* a book, I would read, but I didn't bring any books. Tonight, as we sat around the campfire, someone read a story called "Stone Soup." I'm so hungry that even stone soup sounds good to me. If I ~~know~~ *knew* the recipe, I ~~made~~ *would make* it.

Well, I'm getting tired of holding this flashlight (I wish I ~~would have~~ *had* a regular lamp!), so I think I'll try to fall asleep.

UNIT 24 (pages 119–124)

1

2. had been
3. had found
4. might have been
5. would . . . have seen
6. owned
7. hadn't earned
8. hadn't paid
9. hadn't given
10. wouldn't have survived
11. had gotten
12. could have paid
13. hadn't met
14. might have been
15. would have disapproved
16. had known
17. hadn't agreed
18. would have taken

2

2. We wish Mary Poppins, the new nanny, hadn't demanded two days off a month. We wish she hadn't been so stubborn about it.
3. I wish I had made (some) money from my pictures today. I wish I could have taken Mary Poppins out for tea.
4. We wish Mary Poppins hadn't taken her day off today. We wish she hadn't gone on a magical journey without us.
5. I wish I hadn't stolen Mary Poppins's magic compass tonight. I wish those giant creatures from the four corners of the world hadn't frightened me.
6. We wish Mary Poppins had wanted to stay forever. We wish she hadn't left with the West Wind last night.

3

2. If he hadn't sold candy to train passengers as a boy, he might not have loved model trains as an adult.
3. He would have joined the army in World War I if he hadn't been too young.
4. If his friend Ub hadn't helped him buy a suit, Disney, who was shy, couldn't have met his fiancée's parents.
5. If he had owned the rights to his first cartoon characters, his distributor wouldn't have cheated him.
6. If his art lessons hadn't meant a lot to Disney, he wouldn't have paid for lessons for Disney Studio artists.
7. If a bank hadn't loaned Disney $1.5 million, he couldn't have made *Snow White and the Seven Dwarfs*.
8. If the movie hadn't succeeded, the bank would have taken Disney's home, his studio, and the film.
9. If Disney hadn't died in 1966, he would have seen the opening of the EPCOT Center in Florida.
10. If he hadn't been a genius, he might not have overcome his unhappy childhood.

4

4. would . . . have saved
5. had bought
6. had made
7. would . . . have gone
8. Would . . . have had to
9. hadn't stayed
10. No, you wouldn't have.
11. had called

12. would . . . have told
13. Yes, they would have.
14. had planned
15. would . . . have enjoyed
16. Yes, you would have.

UNIT 25 (pages 125–128)

1

2. they
3. me
4. she
5. was
6. had taken
7. her
8. him
9. 'd gotten
10. don't
11. are
12. they
13. planned
14. he
15. told
16. hadn't committed
17. had scored

2

2. (that) it's Wednesday.
3. (that) her husband had driven her to the interview.
4. (that) their house is near the lake.
5. (that) she'd shoplifted a lipstick once as a teenager.
6. (that) she'd gone to her mother right away.
7. (that) she'd taken her to the store to return the lipstick.
8. (that) she always tells the truth.
9. (that) the test seems easy.
10. (that) she doesn't mind taking lie-detector tests.

3

3. He said (OR told the interviewer) (that) he'd been a salesclerk. That's true.
4. He said (OR told the interviewer) (that) he'd received a promotion to supervisor. That's not true.
5. He said (OR told the interviewer) (that) he'd supervised five other salesclerks. That's not true.
6. He said (OR told the interviewer) (that) he'd been a reliable employee. That's true.
7. He said (OR told the interviewer) (that) he'd shown initiative. That's true.
8. He said (OR told the interviewer) (that) his employers had liked his work. That's true.
9. He said (OR told the interviewer) (that) Bates hadn't fired him. That's true.
10. He said (OR told the interviewer) (that) he'd lost his job because of staff reductions. That's true.
11. He said (OR told the interviewer) (that) he'd earned $25,000 a year. That's not true.
12. He said (OR told the interviewer) (that) he'd gotten a raise of more than $2,000. That's not true.

UNIT 26 (pages 129–133)

1

2. He said (that) he'd been living there his whole life.
3. He said (that) he'd experienced many earthquakes in his years there.
4. He said (that) that quake had been the worst.
5. He said (that) he would start to rebuild his home that week.
6. He said (that) he had to make it stronger.
7. He said (that) he might get government aid the following month.
8. He said (that) he couldn't afford earthquake insurance right then.
9. He said (that) he had looked into it before the earthquake.
10. He said (that) he should have bought some insurance then.

2

2. She said (that) she'd felt a sensation of falling.
3. He said (that) they'd all been pretty well prepared for an earthquake, but not for the fire.
4. He said (that) you can't (OR couldn't) save everyone.
5. He said (that) he hadn't seen anything like it.
6. He said (that) it had felt like a giant hand reaching down and shaking him.
7. She said (that) she was scared that there was going to be another one.
8. She said (that) she was so glad she was there.
9. She said (that) although she'd been through war in her country, she'd had no idea what to do in the quake.
10. She said (that) if they said her house couldn't be saved, she didn't know what she'd do or where she'd go.

3

(Answers may vary slightly.)
3. That's right. She said (that) several thousand of them might occur that day.
4. That's right. She said (that) most would go unnoticed because they'd occur beneath the ocean surface.
5. That's wrong. She acknowledged (that) some had started dangerous tidal waves.

6. That's right. She added that the tsunami had killed hundreds of thousands of people.
7. That's wrong. She stated (that) she couldn't explain in great detail because it would be too complicated.
8. That's wrong. She indicated (that) a hidden fault had caused the 1994 Los Angeles quake.
9. That's right. She noted (that) it had had several strong quakes in the past 20 years.
10. That's right. She said (that) another interviewer had asked her that same question the day before.
11. That's wrong. She claimed (that) scientists might be able to make more accurate predictions sometime in the future.
12. That's right. She said (that) it was a good idea for them to have an emergency plan.

UNIT 27 (pages 134–137)

1

2. She told me not to turn right.
3. "Slow down."
4. "Don't drive so fast."
5. She asked me to turn on the radio.
6. "Can (OR Could) you please open the window?" OR "Please open the window."
7. "Please come in for coffee." OR "Come in for coffee, please." OR "Would you like to come in for coffee?"
8. She told me not to park in the bus stop.

2

3. drivers not to rely on caffeinated beverages such as coffee or cola to stay awake.
4. drivers to share the driving responsibilities with another person if possible.
5. drivers not to wait until they're sleepy to take a break.
6. drivers to stop every couple of hours and stretch their legs by walking around.
7. drivers to listen to music or a book on tape.
8. drivers not to daydream.
9. drivers not to park on the side of the road if they need to stop for a short nap.

3

2. told
3. to slow
4. not to
5. to pull
6. to show
7. ordered
8. to take
9. invited
10. to wait

4

2. (Please) buckle your seat belt.
3. (Please) slow down.
4. (Please) don't speed.
5. (Please) pull over and stop.
6. (Please) show me your license. OR Would you (please) show me your license?
7. (Please) give me the permit.
8. (Please) take the wheel (and follow me to the police station).
9. Would you like to have dinner at my place?
10. Could (OR Can) you wait until another day?

UNIT 28 (pages 138–141)

1

2. She asked (me) whether I had time yesterday.
3. She asked (me) if I could show her some photos.
4. She asked (me) what my full name was.
5. She asked (me) who had chosen my name.
6. She asked (me) when I was born.
7. She asked (me) what country my family had come from.
8. She asked (me) where I was born.
9. She asked (me) what my biggest adventure had been.
10. She asked (me) what I was most proud of.

2

2. how old he had been
3. how much it had cost
4. why he hadn't asked the name of the fruit
5. why the details had seemed so important
6. how they were going to get by
7. if (OR whether) he had some time to talk to him
8. if (OR whether) he felt comfortable there
9. if (OR whether) he remembered their trip to the circus
10. what he had worn to school
11. what his mother had cooked
12. what hobbies he had had
13. what his most important decision had been
14. what new invention he likes (OR liked) best

3

3. He asked her where she had grown up.
4. He didn't ask her why she had moved to San Francisco.
5. He asked her what she had studied.
6. He asked her if (OR whether) she had worked during high school.

7. He asked her if (OR whether) she had ever lived in another country.
8. He asked her if (OR whether) she speaks (OR spoke) other languages.
9. He didn't ask her why she had named her first book *I Know Why the Caged Bird Sings*.
10. He asked her why she had started writing.
11. He didn't ask her if (OR whether) she had studied writing.
12. He asked her where she likes (OR liked) to write.

UNIT 29 (pages 142–146)

1

2. why you enjoy watching sports all the time.
3. how you can watch those boring travel shows.
4. what the most popular travel destinations are.
5. when your last vacation was?
6. if (OR whether) I'm going to take a vacation anytime soon.
7. how you're going to pay for your dream vacation?
8. how much a volunteer vacation will cost.
9. if (OR whether) people really take vacations where they have to work.
10. which organization has volunteer vacations in Africa?
11. where I should go for more information?

2

2. if (OR whether) I have to be over 21 to go on a volunteer vacation.
3. who pays for the trip?
4. what the average cost of a volunteer vacation is?
5. if (OR whether) students on a volunteer vacation should bring any extra money?
6. if (OR whether) I'll have any free time on a volunteer vacation.
7. how long the trips usually last?
8. when most students take volunteer vacations.
9. if (OR whether) most of the volunteer opportunities are in the U.S.?
10. how far in advance I have to plan a volunteer vacation.

3

2. where to look for a nonstop flight and the lowest possible airfare.
3. how to rent a car.
4. what to do about rental car insurance.
5. where to go for an inexpensive language course.
6. how long to stay in Spain.
7. what kind of clothes to pack.
8. who to talk to about hotels and restaurants.

4

I don't know when ~~are you~~ *you are* leaving for your trip, but I decided to write anyway. How are you? Dan and I and the kids are all fine. Busy as usual. Tonight Dan and I got a babysitter and went to the movies (we hardly ever have the chance to go out alone). We saw a romantic comedy called The Wedding Date. I don't know ~~is it~~ *if it's* playing near you, but I recommend it.

I was thinking about the last time we were in San Francisco together. Can you remember where we ate*?* I know the restaurant was somewhere in Chinatown, but I can't remember what it was called.

I've been wondering why I haven't heard from Wu-lan*.* Do you know where ~~did he move~~ *he moved*? I'd like to write to him, but I don't know how to contact him.

Well, the summer is almost here. Let us know when ~~can you~~ *you can* come for a visit. It would be great to see you again.

Test: Units 1–4

PART ONE

Circle the letter of the correct answer to complete each sentence.

Example
Mark _____ a headache last night.   Ⓐ B C D
(A) had   (C) has had
(B) has   (D) was having

1. Water _____ at 0 degrees C.   A B C D
   (A) freezes   (C) has been freezing
   (B) froze   (D) is freezing

2. In our World History class, we _____ about the causes of the Korean War this week.   A B C D
   (A) learn   (C) are learning
   (B) was learning   (D) had learned

3. Sarah _____ glasses since she was a young girl. She can't see anything without them.   A B C D
   (A) wore   (C) is wearing
   (B) has worn   (D) wears

4. John _____. It really annoys me.   A B C D
   (A) always complain   (C) is always complaining
   (B) had always complained   (D) was always complaining

5. Vicki is planning to transfer to another school, but I _____ that she should stay here.   A B C D
   (A) thinking   (C) thought
   (B) 'd thought   (D) think

6. By 11:00 this morning, I _____ three cups of coffee.   A B C D
   (A) drink   (C) had drunk
   (B) had been drinking (D) have drunk

7. I was listening to the radio when I _____ the news.   A B C D
   (A) hear   (C) 've heard
   (B) heard   (D) was hearing

(continued)

T-1

8. Ellen and Jack _____ in Europe when they met for the first time. A B C D

   (A) traveled
   (B) have traveled
   (C) have been traveling
   (D) were traveling

9. We have been studying English grammar _____ six months. A B C D

   (A) for
   (B) since
   (C) already
   (D) after

10. Can you please turn down the TV? The baby _____. A B C D

   (A) has slept
   (B) is sleeping
   (C) sleeps
   (D) slept

11. The Morrisons _____ to Texas last September. A B C D

   (A) had moved
   (B) have been moving
   (C) have moved
   (D) moved

12. While Jedd was living in Toronto, Helen _____ in California. A B C D

   (A) was living
   (B) had lived
   (C) lives
   (D) has lived

PART TWO

Each sentence has four underlined words or phrases. The four underlined parts of the sentence are marked A, B, C, and D. Circle the letter of the <u>one</u> underlined word or phrase that is NOT CORRECT.

Example
Rosa <u>rarely</u> <u>is using</u> public transportation, but <u>today</u> she <u>is taking</u> the bus. A (B) C D
     A   B   C   D

13. The doctor <u>called</u> <u>this morning</u> <u>while</u> you <u>slept</u>. A B C D
                A   B   C   D

14. <u>When</u> the students <u>arrived</u>, their teacher <u>was giving</u> them an assignment A B C D
    A   B   C

    because they <u>needed</u> additional practice.
                       D

15. I'm really hungry because I <u>haven't had</u> lunch <u>yet</u>, but I <u>wait</u> for my friends A B C D
                                   A   B   C

    because I <u>want</u> to eat with them.
            D

16. <u>By the time</u> I <u>had gotten</u> home, the show <u>had</u> <u>already</u> ended. A B C D
      A   B   C   D

17. Pete and Andy <u>were driving</u> to work <u>when</u> they <u>were seeing</u> the accident. A B C D
               A   B   C   D

18. Erika <u>has</u> <u>been looking</u> for a job <u>since</u> she <u>has graduated</u> from college. A B C D
      A   B   C   D

19. Janice didn't <u>own</u> a car then because she <u>hasn't</u> <u>learned</u> to drive <u>yet</u>. A B C D
              A   B   C   D

20. I <u>had</u> <u>been living</u> in this apartment for ten years, but <u>I'm</u> <u>looking</u> for a new A B C D
    A   B   C   D

    one now.

Test: Units 5–6

PART ONE

Circle the letter of the correct answer to complete each sentence.

Example
Mark _____ a headache last night. (Ⓐ B C D)
- (A) had
- (B) has
- (C) has had
- (D) was having

1. Bill will be _____ to Taipei tomorrow. A B C D
   - (A) flies
   - (B) flying
   - (C) fly
   - (D) have been flying

2. We _____ a new TV soon. A B C D
   - (A) own
   - (B) 'll own
   - (C) 're owning
   - (D) 'll have owned

3. Look at those dark clouds! It _____. A B C D
   - (A) rains
   - (B) 's going to rain
   - (C) 's raining
   - (D) will rain

4. They'll be making photocopies while he _____ typing the report. A B C D
   - (A) finishes
   - (B) 'll be finishing
   - (C) 'll finish
   - (D) 's been finishing

5. I _____ be working tomorrow. I'll be out of town. A B C D
   - (A) don't
   - (B) haven't
   - (C) 'm not
   - (D) won't

6. Kareem will _____ almost $1,000 by next year. A B C D
   - (A) had saved
   - (B) have been saving
   - (C) have saved
   - (D) saves

7. We're late. When we _____ there, they'll already have eaten dinner. A B C D
   - (A) get
   - (B) got
   - (C) 'll get
   - (D) 'll have gotten

8. By the end of this week, Henry _____ regularly for six months. A B C D
   - (A) exercised
   - (B) exercises
   - (C) will exercise
   - (D) will have been exercising

(continued)

T-3

9. When I finish this story by Nguyen Treng, I'll _____ all of her mysteries.   A B C D

   (A) be reading   (C) have read
   (B) have been reading   (D) read

10. Next year, the Carters will have moved to their new house _____.   A B C D

    (A) already   (C) since
    (B) for   (D) yet

PART TWO

Each sentence has four underlined words or phrases. The four underlined parts of the sentence are marked A, B, C, and D. Circle the letter of the one underlined word or phrase that is NOT CORRECT.

Example
Rosa <u>rarely</u> <u>is using</u> public transportation, but <u>today</u> she <u>is taking</u> the bus.   A (B) C D
     A   B   C   D

11. <u>Will</u> you <u>been</u> <u>going</u> to the supermarket <u>tonight</u>?   A B C D

12. <u>While</u> Bill <u>will wash</u> the dishes, <u>I'll</u> be <u>sweeping</u> the floor.   A B C D

13. <u>By the time</u> I <u>got</u> home, <u>I'll have</u> <u>walked</u> three miles and I'll be ready for   A B C D
    a big breakfast.

14. Professor Sanek <u>will have</u> <u>returned</u> to the office by 4:00, and he <u>calls</u>   A B C D
    you <u>then</u>.

15. The Lees <u>will save</u> <u>for</u> ten years <u>by the time</u> their first child <u>enters</u> college.   A B C D

16. Ana will <u>has</u> <u>been</u> watching TV <u>for</u> an hour by the time dinner <u>is</u> ready.   A B C D

17. In the near future, most people in this country <u>will</u> <u>be</u> <u>work</u> in service jobs   A B C D
    after they <u>complete</u> their education.

18. At the end of this year, Tania <u>will</u> <u>be</u> free of debt because she will <u>already</u>   A B C D
    have <u>been paying</u> her entire credit card bill.

19. Tania <u>will</u> <u>have spent</u> $1,000 in interest <u>before</u> she <u>will pay off</u> her loan.   A B C D

20. John loves that old suitcase. By the time he <u>gets</u> home from vacation   A B C D
    <u>next month</u>, he'll <u>have</u> <u>carries</u> it at least 50,000 miles.

Test: Units 7–8

PART ONE

Circle the letter of the correct answer to complete each sentence.

Example
Mark _____ a headache last night.   (Ⓐ) B C D
(A) had   (C) has had
(B) has   (D) was having

1. _____ you from Panama?   A B C D
   (A) Aren't   (C) Did
   (B) Come   (D) Didn't

2. Ben's not at work today, _____?   A B C D
   (A) does he   (C) is he
   (B) doesn't he   (D) isn't he

3. Your cousin lived in New York, _____?   A B C D
   (A) didn't she   (C) isn't she
   (B) hadn't she   (D) wasn't she

4. Miguel _____ here very long, has he?   A B C D
   (A) has been   (C) was
   (B) hasn't been   (D) wasn't

5. — Doesn't Sam own a house in Florida?   A B C D
   — _____ He bought one there last year.
   (A) No, he doesn't. (C) Yes, he does.
   (B) No, he didn't. (D) Yes, he did.

6. — Can't Rick speak Spanish?   A B C D
   — _____ He never learned.
   (A) No, he can't.   (C) Yes, he can.
   (B) No, he doesn't. (D) Yes, he does.

(continued)

7. That's your notebook, isn't _____?

   (A) there
   (B) it
   (C) yours
   (D) that

8. — You're not Alex, are you?
   — _____ I'm Alex Winslow.

   (A) No, I'm not.
   (B) No, you're not.
   (C) Yes, I am.
   (D) Yes, you are.

9. — Today's July 5th, isn't it?
   — _____ It's the 6th.

   (A) Neither is it.
   (B) No, it isn't.
   (C) So is it.
   (D) Yes, it is.

10. They've read the paper, _____ I have too.

    (A) and
    (B) but
    (C) either
    (D) neither

11. — Jennifer ate at home last night.
    — _____ I saw him having dinner at Manny's Diner.

    (A) But Mike did.
    (B) But Mike didn't.
    (C) Neither did Mike.
    (D) So did Mike.

12. — Andrea speaks fluent French.
    — _____

    (A) Neither does Paul.
    (B) So does Paul.
    (C) So is Paul.
    (D) So Paul does.

13. — I won't be at Judy's party next week.
    — Neither _____, and it's too bad. It's going to be a great party.

    (A) I will
    (B) will I
    (C) am I
    (D) I'll be

14. The hotel _____ expensive, and so were the restaurants.

    (A) was
    (B) wasn't
    (C) were
    (D) weren't

PART TWO

Each sentence has four underlined words or phrases. The four underlined parts of the sentence are marked A, B, C, and D. Circle the letter of the one underlined word or phrase that is NOT CORRECT.

Example
Rosa <u>rarely</u> <u>is using</u> public transportation, but <u>today</u> she <u>is taking</u> the bus.   A (B) C D
     A   B   C   D

15. <u>This</u> <u>isn't</u> the way to Route 101, <u>is</u> <u>this</u>?   A B C D
    A   B   C D

16. Mary isn't <u>working</u> on Saturday <u>morning</u>, <u>isn't</u> <u>she</u>?   A B C D
                   A   B   C D

17. Jeff <u>bought</u> a new car, <u>and</u> <u>so</u> <u>does</u> Ann.   A B C D
       A   B C D

18. Rachel <u>didn't</u> <u>go</u> to class today, <u>and</u> her sister <u>did</u>.   A B C D
         A B   C   D

19. I <u>didn't enjoy</u> the movie, <u>and</u> Frank <u>did</u> <u>either</u>.   A B C D
     A   B   C D

20. Vilma <u>is coming</u> to the movies with us, <u>and</u> <u>so</u> <u>Craig is</u>.   A B C D
         A   B C D

Test: Units 9–10

PART ONE

Circle the letter of the correct answer to complete each sentence.

Example
Mark _____ a headache last night.   Ⓐ B C D

(A) had (C) has had
(B) has (D) was having

1. _____ the streets safe again is the mayor's highest priority.   A B C D

   (A) Is making (C) Makes
   (B) Make (D) Making

2. Geraldo is looking forward to _____ a father.   A B C D

   (A) became (C) becomes
   (B) becoming (D) become

3. It was very difficult _____ a good job.   A B C D

   (A) find (C) has found
   (B) found (D) to find

4. Elliot bought an exercise video _____ him get into shape.   A B C D

   (A) helped (C) help
   (B) helps (D) to help

5. It's time _____ where we want to go this summer.   A B C D

   (A) to decide (C) deciding
   (B) decides (D) decide

6. I'm sorry, but I forgot _____ that book you asked for.   A B C D

   (A) bring (C) to bring
   (B) bringing (D) brought

7. I can't imagine _____ that.   A B C D

   (A) do (C) you to do
   (B) to do (D) your doing

8. Pat invited _____ the weekend with them.   A B C D

   (A) to spend (C) me to spend
   (B) me spend (D) my spending

T-8

9. The judge made the witness _____ the question.   A B C D
   (A) answer   (C) answering
   (B) answered   (D) to answer

10. Because the restaurant is so popular, I suggest _____ a reservation.   A B C D
    (A) make   (C) makes
    (B) making   (D) to make

11. I studied a lot, so I expected _____ the test.   A B C D
    (A) passed   (C) pass
    (B) passing   (D) to pass

12. Most teachers won't let their students _____ a dictionary during an exam.   A B C D
    (A) use   (C) using
    (B) to use   (D) are using

PART TWO

Each sentence has four underlined words or phrases. The four underlined parts of the sentence are marked A, B, C, and D. Circle the letter of the one underlined word or phrase that is NOT CORRECT.

Example
Rosa <u>rarely</u> <u>is using</u> public transportation, but <u>today</u> she <u>is taking</u> the bus.   A (B) C D
    A   B   C   D

13. I <u>got</u> all my friends <u>help</u> <u>me</u> <u>move</u> last June.   A B C D

14. Phil decided <u>changing</u> jobs because his boss always <u>made</u> <u>him</u> <u>work</u> late.   A B C D

15. The students of Maitlin High <u>appreciated</u> their <u>principal's</u> <u>try</u> <u>to improve</u> conditions in their school.   A B C D

16. Because she wants <u>to be</u> a good boss, Sally can't help <u>to feel</u> responsible for <u>everyone's</u> <u>doing</u> the work on time.   A B C D

17. Robert <u>succeeded in</u> <u>to find</u> a job after high school, so his parents <u>didn't make</u> him <u>apply</u> to college.   A B C D

18. If you insist <u>on</u> <u>looking</u> over the report, please <u>remember</u> <u>returning</u> it by Monday.   A B C D

19. <u>Going</u> on a diet doesn't <u>seem</u> <u>to be</u> the best way <u>losing</u> weight.   A B C D

20. Because my husband was <u>planning</u> <u>to go</u> to the post office, I <u>asked him</u> <u>mail</u> a package for me.   A B C D

Test: Units 11–12

PART ONE

Circle the letter of the correct answer to complete each sentence.

Example
Mark _____ a headache last night.   (A) B C D

(A) had (C) has had
(B) has (D) was having

1. Jan is my best friend. I can always count _____ her.   A B C D

   (A) for (C) on
   (B) with (D) out

2. Your mother called. She wants you to call her _____ tonight.   A B C D

   (A) back (C) off
   (B) in (D) over

3. That's very original. How did you dream _____ that idea?   A B C D

   (A) about (C) of
   (B) down (D) up

4. — It's cold outside. You need your jacket.
   — OK. I'll put _____.   A B C D

   (A) it on (C) on it
   (B) it over (D) over it

5. Some damage was brought _____ by high winds.   A B C D

   (A) about (C) down
   (B) across (D) through

6. Come in. Please sit _____.   A B C D

   (A) down (C) it down
   (B) down it (D) up

7. Every spring, Marta _____ away some clothes to a local charity.   A B C D

   (A) gives (C) puts
   (B) keeps (D) throws

8. I can hardly hear the TV. Could you turn it _____?   A B C D

   (A) in (C) on
   (B) off (D) up

9. She ran _____ on the way to the supermarket.   A B C D
   (A) him into
   (B) into
   (C) into Jason
   (D) Jason into

10. It's too cold to take your gloves off. _____   A B C D
    (A) Keep on.
    (B) Keep them.
    (C) Keep on them.
    (D) Keep them on.

11. Erika wants to quit, but she says she'll _____.   A B C D
    (A) give up
    (B) see the project through
    (C) see through the project
    (D) see through it

PART TWO

Each sentence has four underlined words or phrases. The four underlined parts of the sentence are marked A, B, C, and D. Circle the letter of the one underlined word or phrase that is NOT CORRECT.

Example
Rosa <u>rarely</u> <u>is using</u> public transportation, but <u>today</u> she <u>is taking</u> the bus.   A (B) C D
    A   B   C   D

12. Could we talk <u>over it</u> before you <u>turn</u> <u>the whole idea</u> <u>down</u>?   A B C D
                    A   B   C   D

13. I <u>let</u> <u>Andy</u> <u>down</u> when I forgot to pick his suit <u>out</u> from the cleaner's.   A B C D
      A   B   C   D

14. After Joanne's boss <u>looked</u> <u>over her proposal</u> to redesign the company's   A B C D
                               A   B
    website, he decided to <u>go along</u> <u>her ideas with</u>.
                            C   D

15. After I <u>hand</u> <u>in</u> <u>my report</u>, I'll take all these books <u>on</u> to the library.   A B C D
            A   B   C   D

16. If you can't <u>figure</u> <u>the meaning of a word that you read out</u>, it's a good idea   A B C D
                   A   B
    to <u>look</u> <u>it up</u> in a dictionary.
        C   D

17. Even a difficult project will <u>turn out</u> well if you <u>come up</u> <u>to an organized plan</u>   A B C D
                             A   B   C
    and stick <u>to it</u>.
          D

18. Instead of <u>calling</u> <u>off</u> the meeting, let's just <u>put it</u> <u>over</u> until next week.   A B C D
             A   B   C   D

19. If you don't use <u>out</u> the milk by Monday, please <u>throw</u> <u>it</u> <u>away</u>.   A B C D
                A   B C   D

20. Greg <u>called up</u> Yuan to <u>cheer up her</u> after her English professor told her to   A B C D
          A   B
    <u>do her research paper</u> <u>over</u>.
         C   D

Test: Units 13–14

PART ONE

*Circle the letter of the correct answer to complete each sentence. Choose (———) when the sentence does not need a relative pronoun or **when**.*

Example
Mark _____ a headache last night.   Ⓐ B C D

(A) had
(B) has
(C) has had
(D) was having

1. Our family home, _____ my grandfather built, was on a busy corner.   A B C D

   (A) where
   (B) which
   (C) whose
   (D) that

2. Lisa, _____ I've already mentioned, wrote me a letter.   A B C D

   (A) which
   (B) whom
   (C) that
   (D) ———

3. Those are the people _____ I told you about.   A B C D

   (A) where
   (B) which
   (C) whose
   (D) ———

4. Do you remember the day _____ we found that old bookstore?   A B C D

   (A) where
   (B) whose
   (C) whom
   (D) when

5. Can you hand me the book _____ is on the top shelf?   A B C D

   (A) that
   (B) where
   (C) who
   (D) ———

6. Do you know the man _____ sister works in the library?   A B C D

   (A) that
   (B) which
   (C) who
   (D) whose

7. Mr. Jay, _____ owns the hardware store, comes from my hometown.   A B C D

   (A) that
   (B) who
   (C) whom
   (D) whose

8. Tell me about the city _____ you grew up.   A B C D
   (A) that   (C) which
   (B) where   (D) ──────

9. Tony loved the book _____ I lent him.   A B C D
   (A) when   (C) whose
   (B) who   (D) ──────

10. The Louvre, _____ is a world-famous museum, is located in Paris.   A B C D
    (A) that   (C) who
    (B) which   (D) ──────

11. The candidate for _____ I voted lost the election.   A B C D
    (A) that   (C) who
    (B) which   (D) whom

12. I often think back on the time _____ we traveled together.   A B C D
    (A) where   (C) who
    (B) which   (D) ──────

PART TWO

Each sentence has four underlined words or phrases. The four underlined parts of the sentence are marked A, B, C, and D. Circle the letter of the one underlined word or phrase that is NOT CORRECT.

Example
Rosa <u>rarely</u> <u>is using</u> public transportation, but <u>today</u> she <u>is taking</u> the bus.   A (B) C D
    A   B   C   D

13. The woman <u>who</u> <u>she</u> <u>lives</u> next door <u>is</u> very nice.   A B C D
               A   B   C   D

14. One <u>singer</u> <u>who's</u> voice <u>I</u> <u>like</u> is Mary Grant.   A B C D
     A   B   C D

15. The <u>stories</u> <u>what</u> <u>are in this book</u> <u>have</u> wonderful illustrations.   A B C D
     A   B   C   D

16. I <u>enjoyed</u> reading the article <u>that</u> you <u>told</u> me about <u>it</u>.   A B C D
  A   B   C   D

17. I've read some <u>books</u> <u>that</u> <u>discusses</u> the time <u>when</u> this area was undeveloped.   A B C D
                    A   B   C   D

18. <u>San Francisco</u>, <u>that</u> <u>is</u> a beautiful <u>city</u>, has a very diverse population.   A B C D
    A   B C   D

19. Do you know the name of the person <u>whom</u> wrote the <u>song</u> <u>that</u> Al <u>was singing</u> last night?   A B C D
                                    A   B   C   D

20. That's the man <u>whose</u> sister <u>work</u> in the store <u>that</u> <u>is</u> on Fifth Street.   A B C D
               A   B   C D

Answer Key for Tests

Correct responses for Part Two questions appear in parentheses.

UNITS 1–4

Part One
1. A
2. C
3. B
4. C
5. D
6. C
7. B
8. D
9. A
10. B
11. D
12. A

Part Two
13. D (were sleeping)
14. C (gave)
15. C ('m waiting)
16. B (got)
17. D (saw)
18. D (graduated)
19. B (hadn't)
20. A (have)

UNITS 5–6

Part One
1. B
2. B
3. B
4. A
5. D
6. C
7. A
8. D
9. C
10. A

Part Two
11. B (be)
12. B (washes)
13. B (get)
14. C ('ll call OR 's going to call OR 'll be calling)
15. A (will have been saving OR will have saved)
16. A (have)
17. C (working)
18. D (paid)
19. D (pays off)
20. D (carried)

UNITS 7–8

Part One
1. A
2. C
3. A
4. B
5. C
6. A
7. B
8. C
9. B
10. A
11. B
12. B
13. B
14. A

Part Two
15. D (it)
16. C (is)
17. D (did)
18. C (but)
19. C (didn't)
20. D (is Craig)

UNITS 9–10

Part One
1. D
2. B
3. D
4. D
5. A
6. C
7. D
8. C
9. A
10. B
11. D
12. A

Part Two
13. B (to help)
14. A (to change)
15. C (trying)
16. B (feeling)
17. B (finding)
18. D (to return)
19. D (of losing OR to lose)
20. D (to mail)

UNITS 11–12

Part One
1. C
2. A
3. D
4. A
5. A
6. A
7. A
8. D
9. C
10. D
11. B

Part Two
12. A (it over)
13. D (up)
14. D (with her ideas)
15. D (back OR over)
16. B (out the meaning of a word that you read)
17. C (with an organized plan)
18. D (off)
19. A (up)
20. B (cheer her up)

UNITS 13–14

Part One
1. B
2. B
3. D
4. D
5. A
6. D
7. B
8. B
9. D
10. B
11. D
12. D

Part Two
13. B (*delete* she)
14. B (whose)
15. B (that OR which)
16. D (*delete* it)
17. C (discuss)
18. B (which)
19. A (who OR that)
20. B (works)